Supporting Pupils on the Autism Spectrum in Primary Schools

Written to meet the needs of teaching assistants and learning support assistants, this book provides a practical toolkit for supporting students on the autism spectrum in mainstream primary schools.

The book offers a clear, jargon-free explanation of autism spectrum conditions and examines the difficulties arising from these conditions and how they can impact on students' learning. Addressing issues that arise on a daily basis, it is full of practical advice and strategies for supporting students socially and academically across all areas of the curriculum.

Features include:

- advice on supporting students through examinations;
- examples and case studies to illustrate how the strategies described work in practice;
- forms to help with information collection and evaluation; and
- templates to scaffold students' comprehension and learning in different subject areas.

Packed with photocopiable resources that can be adapted to suit individual students' needs, this book is essential reading for teaching assistants who want to help their students on the autism spectrum to reach their full potential.

Cary Canavan is a Consultant in Autism specialising in Asperger Syndrome. She offers training, advice and support for those teaching and employing young people with AS.

Supporting Pupils on the Autism Spectrum in Primary Schools

A Practical Guide for Teaching Assistants

Cary Canavan

Routledge
Taylor & Francis Group

LONDON AND NEW YORK

First published 2016
by Routledge
2 Park Square, Milton Park, Abingdon, Oxon OX14 4RN

and by Routledge
711 Third Avenue, New York, NY 10017

Routledge is an imprint of the Taylor & Francis Group, an informa business

British Library Cataloguing in Publication Data
A catalogue record for this book is available from the British Library

Library of Congress Cataloging in Publication Data
Canavan, Carolyn
Supporting pupils on the autism spectrum in primary schools : a practical guide for teaching assistants / Cary Canavan.
pages cm
Includes bibliographical references.
1. Autistic children--Education (Primary)--Handbooks, manuals, etc. 2. Teachers' assistants--Handbooks, manuals, etc. I. Title.
LC4717.C359 2015
371.94--dc23
2015002446

ISBN: 978-1-138-83889-5 (hbk)
ISBN: 978-1-138-83888-8 (pbk)
ISBN: 978-1-315-73373-9 (ebk)

Typeset in Helvetica
by Saxon Graphics Ltd, Derby

Printed and bound by CPI Group (UK) Ltd, Croydon, CR0 4YY

Contents

How to use this book

The book is split into three parts:

Part One: Asperger Syndrome: the basic physiology, and how it can impact upon a person's life, together with a brief history of the condition.

Part Two: how the school's social and physical environment can impact upon the pupil's behaviour, and ways to manage it. It is critical to prepare for the pupil before they arrive. This section lays down the foundations for a smooth transition into primary school; explores the reason for a pupil's behaviour; and how to react in a crisis and avoid one altogether. The younger child with an ASC is less able to regulate their nervous system and control their emotions. This means that the behavioural challenges facing them on a daily basis are greater.

Part Three: subject areas; the difficulties they present and strategies, including photocopiable templates, to support your target pupils across the curriculum. In the primary school much of the learning is already supported by visual references and worksheets. Language modification and differentiation may help the pupil with AS to achieve beyond their years. The challenge for teachers and TAs is to send them to secondary school self-confident enough to continue to progress.

The book builds upon the need for consistency and clear instructions to support the pupil across the curriculum by reducing the number of different ways to do the same thing, and maintaining clarity of language so that the pupil understands exactly what is expected of them.

Most chapters contain an explanation of how autism, a neurological developmental disorder, affects the topic, be it behaviour or learning. This is followed by a discussion, practical advice, detailed description of strategies, and templates to enable you to support them effectively in lessons.

There is a comprehensive reading list of books and website addresses exploring the issues in greater depth at the end of each topic chapter. I have read all the books and chosen them for their usefulness and readability. The most insightful are written by people on the spectrum and these are italicised.

Autism is a heterogeneous condition: no two people with the condition are the same. A strategy or intervention that works with one child may not work with another. Therefore, you should learn about each individual and how you can support them effectively in school. Find out about their unique autistic operating system.

Autism is also largely a hidden condition. The pupil with a diagnosis of an ASC, regardless of having an Education Health and Care Plan (EHCP), has several basic needs and these are best met by putting together an Individual Education Plan that includes the following principles:

1 Maintain consistency at all times – avoid changes when possible.
2 Prepare for any changes – staff, room, timetable, groups – well in advance.
3 Have strategies in place from the start, which all staff dealing with the pupil apply without deviation.

4 Expectations of behaviour and working practices should be consistent from lesson to lesson, room to room, staff member to staff member.

If the pupils know what is expected of them, they can meet those needs and feel safe and competent. Change leads to confusion, fear having a profound effect upon the pupil's self-esteem. Knowledge of the impact of autism, understanding of the pupil's needs, tolerance and a genuine regard for the individual will enable you to support them to do the best they can. They will not disappoint you.

Accept $\approx$ Respect $\approx$ Protect

Note on the terms: Autistic Spectrum Conditions and Asperger Syndrome

According to the National Autistic Society (NAS): 'The term 'autism' is used to describe all diagnoses on the autism spectrum including classic autism, Asperger syndrome and high-functioning autism.'

However, in 2013 in the 5th edition of the Diagnostic and Statistical Manual of Mental Disorders, (DSM 5) published by the American Psychiatric Association (APA), Asperger Syndrome (AS) has been absorbed into the term Autistic Spectrum Disorders (otherwise known as Autistic Spectrum Conditions – ASC). It continues to exist in the World Health Organisation's (WHO) International Classification of Diseases (ICD 10).

ASC is more popular as a term among academics than ASD because it is less stigmatising and acknowledges that, while individuals have been diagnosed as having disabilities, they also have areas of strengths in thinking, imagining, reasoning, learning, understanding and memory. Both individuals with High Functioning Autism (HFA) and AS have average to high IQs and people with AS have no delay in language although it may be stilted and idiosyncratic.

However, Asperger Syndrome is still classified as a separate term by the NAS, which is a primary resource here in the UK; so I use the term Asperger Syndrome (AS) and Autism Spectrum Conditions (ASC) interchangeably throughout the book.

Introduction

Staff supporting pupils on the autism spectrum in mainstream primary schools are often there at the start of the journey. You are invaluable to our children. You are interpreters, guardians and advocates. This book is for you. I hope the practical strategies and templates in this book will help you support your pupils and teachers across the curriculum.

I am an ex-English teacher with Special Educational Needs (SEN) teaching experience in primary and secondary schools. My son was diagnosed with Asperger Syndrome (AS) at the age of 13. When I realised he was autistic, two years before he was diagnosed, I resolved to learn as much as I could about the condition (a lifetime project). While studying for my masters degree in autism at the University of Birmingham, I took a job as a teaching assistant (TA) in a mainstream secondary school supporting pupils with AS.

However, while working as an SEN teacher in a primary school overseas, I had the privilege of working with a 9-year-old 'gifted child', who had Asperger Syndrome (undiagnosed). It was my job to challenge him. We learned Latin, French, studied Shakespeare and Chaucer. He was quite extraordinary. When he went to do the entrance exam for a scholarship to the top independent school in the country, he didn't do the English essay because the topics were 'boring'. Luckily, I told him to take the book he had written with him to show the principal.

At least 1 in 100 children are diagnosed with an Autistic Spectrum Condition (ASC) and 71 per cent of these are now educated in mainstream schools. Only 22 per cent of teachers have been trained specifically in ASCs, typically for 1 to 4 hours. Ideally, each school should have an autism base with specially trained staff to support the AS pupils and a continuous programme of training for all teachers in ASCs.

The reality is that the child with an ASC is simply another pupil on the SEN register and is supported, or not, by members of the SEN team, who may or may not have been trained or understand the condition and its impact on learning and behaviour. However, in my experience, TAs are going on the courses, and sometimes know more about ASCs than teachers.

Using the square peg (autistic) round peg (neuro-typical: NT) analogy: mainstream schools have lots of round holes; some may be different sizes to accommodate a range of round pegs but, basically, they are all round holes. Square pegs do not fit into round holes, unless you shave off the corners and knock them in. Doing this, you damage the square peg. It looks round but it isn't. If you have square pegs make square holes into which they can fit easily or, at the very least, make the round holes larger.

Many educators advocate the latter, believing that children with ASCs need to learn how to fit into the NT (non-autistic) world. Autistic children will become autistic adults. They may learn how to manage themselves but only in an autism friendly environment. They still suffer extreme stress and can meltdown or shutdown when overloaded. This doesn't change whether they are aged 4, 14 or 40.

The purpose of this book is to explain, in layman's terms, why pupils with an ASC have difficulties with learning and social skills and display idiosyncratic behaviours. Issues are discussed, followed by detailed advice, strategies and the tools to implement them. These are not exhaustive and I hope that you will read some of the recommended texts and develop your own strategies, tailoring them to the needs of the individual pupil you work with.

By the time you finish this book and are practised in using the strategies, I hope the support you give your ASC pupils will be underpinned by an understanding of why the child with AS behaves this way; the difficulties they face; and how you might support them with strategies and resources appropriate to the individual child.

Thank you for reading this book. I infer from this that you are interested in children like my son, and care enough to seek ways to help them achieve the best they can. Our children quite literally change the world, for all their difficulties.

Part One

1 Strengths of individuals with Asperger Syndrome or High Functioning Autism

Before I talk about their difficulties, I would like to write about some of their strengths:

- The individual with AS/HFA is loyal and socially optimistic: they will persevere with a friendship, even if let down.
- They are free from prejudice and accept people at face value.
- Contrary to popular belief, they are very empathic and may surprise you with their insight. (They just don't know what to do about another person's feelings.)
- They will tell you what they really feel and think about something rather than what they think you want to hear.
- When they ask a question – they want the honest answer to it. There is no hidden motive behind it.
- They will tell the truth even if it means getting themselves in trouble.
- They rarely do something they know to be wrong, even when pressured.
- They have a strong sense of justice and neither fear nor favour.
- Their humour can be unique and unconventional.
- They love words, especially puns, and will make up their own jokes with them.
- They want to co-operate but often don't know how.
- If they enjoy a sport, they will train hard to be the best and are particularly good at individual sports.
- They have the ability to learn quickly and want to progress, especially if interested in the topic.
- When they start a task they want to do it perfectly.
- They have a good eye for detail and pick up mistakes.
- If it interests them, they can concentrate on a single task for a very long period of time.
- When they are interested or motivated in a task they will persevere with an extraordinary determination to finish.
- Their long-term memory is good, especially for childhood experiences, facts, figures, dates and film dialogue or audio recordings.
- They are creative, often insightful, and can provide an original solution to a problem.
- Their spatial awareness can be quite remarkable – they are visual thinkers.
- They often have an encyclopaedic knowledge of their special interest.
- Of average or above average intelligence, they have the potential to go on to university.
- They often have an interest or a talent for something: design, Japanese, quantum physics, art, music or computing – find out and nurture it.

2 Important things to know about Autism Spectrum Conditions

The Autism Spectrum covers a very broad range of Pervasive Developmental Disorders, which are life-long neuro-physiological conditions (see glossary for descriptions of each of these conditions):

- Classic Autism, also known as Kanner Syndrome or Low Functioning Autism;
- High Functioning Autism (HFA);
- Asperger Syndrome (AS);
- Semantic Pragmatic Disorder (SPD);
- Pathological Demand Avoidance Syndrome (PDA);
- Retts Syndrome;
- Tourette Syndrome;
- Pervasive Development Disorder Not Otherwise Specified (PDD-NOS) – this often develops into autism or AS later in life, or a child with autism may improve and be re-diagnosed with PDD-NOS.

Most ASCs are hidden disabilities caused by differences in the formation of the brain and the way it responds to stimuli. This is backed up by research using *functional Magnetic Resonance Imaging (*fMRI) scans, which detects blood flow through the brain in response to a variety of stimuli. Consequently, our expectations of individuals with an ASC can sometimes be compared to asking a blind person to 'look at this' or a deaf person to 'listen'; this is why it is so important that we understand the condition and appreciate the difficulties they are confronted with on a daily basis.

Research into autism is ongoing and new findings occur on a regular basis. The brains of individuals with Asperger Syndrome are bigger than average and they have more white and grey matter. Grey matter is responsible for extracting and processing information from sensory organs such as sight, sound and speech, and is involved in muscle control, memory and emotions. Various parts of the brain compare that information with what's in the memory and use the information to plan and execute behaviour. White matter carries information around the brain through electric and chemical activity, but this is also disordered.

More recent research suggests that the autistic brain has more neural pathways to carry information round the brain but that they are not co-ordinated, or that the white matter is too short so that the brain's neural pathways are under-connected. Or that more information comes into the brain than it is able to process, leading to overload. In order to function, people with autism use strategies to distract themselves from the stimuli that threaten to overwhelm them, leading to a display of idiosyncratic behaviours. Researchers concluded that this might explain the problems with attention: for example, if too much information comes in through the visual system, they become distracted and show less interest in social interaction. However, they also suggest that hyper-connectivity might explain the islets of ability in subjects and visual search or detailed focus processing.

Whatever the current theory, it is enough to know that autistic brains work differently.

Difficulties processing information

As a result of all these differences, people with an ASC have processing difficulties affecting:

- social interaction;
- emotional recognition and regulation;
- impulse suppression;
- language processing – input and output;
- fine and gross motor skills;
- planning and organization;
- attention, short term memory;
- the ability to be flexible;
- sensory regulation.

There may also be areas of profound ability in any subject area: not just science or maths and music or art.

To use a metaphor to illustrate the problem:

1 The typical brain is like a road network. Information coming in at A goes to B by travelling along the neural pathways. Like a car travelling along the motorways, the information gets to its destination without any fuss.
2 The autistic brain is different. Information coming in at A goes to B, but it takes longer, like a car going from A to B along detours. It may even get lost and end up at the seaside (C) for a holiday, turning up at its destination weeks or even months later.
3 With the uneven distribution of grey and white matter, and the low levels of chemical neurotransmitters to push inhibitory messages across the synapses (joints), it may even be a more arduous journey, with traffic jams and detours. The synapses may even be broken in some places so that processing is impaired and takes much longer.
4 The uneven distribution of white and grey matter may account for the exceptional abilities one can find in pupils with AS, such as calculating complex mathematical equations without the apparent need to process them, or a photographic memory by which large amounts of text can be quoted but with little comprehension. Like a shortcut, getting from A to B without really knowing how – it's just the way they have always done it.

    Faulty connections may also account for sensory issues. Super-efficient neural pathways may cause hypersensitivity and a flood of information, so that the nervous system is constantly under pressure to process more than it can; and the lack of connectedness, together with thin white matter and patchy grey matter, can be the cause of hyposensitivity.

Processing tasks: planning and writing an essay has been described to me as like building a tower of cards – 'it's very hard'! An interruption by a well-meaning TA or teacher sends the tower tumbling down. They have to start all over again because of a poor working memory. How frustrating is that! You will see an upset and angry child.

The amygdala

The amygdala (there are two) are a small part of the brain that have a major influence on much of the behaviour of a child on the spectrum; they are responsible for recognizing and co-ordinating information from different parts of the brain and processing an emotional response. It is one of the areas in the brain responsible for recognizing social cues such as facial expressions and body language: the emotional responses of other people. In the early years the amygdala are enlarged in people with an ASC, but they shrink to become smaller than normal in adolescence.

The amygdala trigger the flight or fight reflex. They are linked to the frontal cerebral cortex via the hypothalamus, which, depending on the information relayed, will suppress the reflex. For example, you see someone baring their teeth at you; your heart races, muscles tense, you feel hot and your hands sweat. These physical reactions are relayed via the hypothalamus to the pre-frontal cortex, which regulates the emotion on a subconscious level in nanoseconds.

At the same time, the cerebral cortex and hippocampus evaluate the information, based upon knowledge or memories of similar past experiences to make a judgement as whether or not there is a threat present. This information is relayed back to the amygdala through two inhibitory neurotransmitters called serotonin and glycine. The rational frontal lobe system overrides the basic instinct of the amygdala. If your brain reasons that the person is actually threatening you, you acknowledge that you are frightened and in danger and run in the opposite direction. If you recognize that he is smiling, your brain suppresses the desire to run away.

The 'faulty wiring' in the brain of children on the autism spectrum, connecting the amygdala to the frontal lobe, where impulses are controlled, may lead to a breakdown in communication. The autistic individual may be unaware of what is really happening. For example, after getting a fright from hearing a loud, unexpected noise, an adrenaline surge causes a racing heart and hyper-alertness to everything around about. The difference is that in a nanosecond NTs assess the danger and quickly realise that it's actually not going to hurt them. There is nothing to be alarmed about, the heart rate returns to normal and the child calms down quickly, although it takes 4 hours for adrenaline to clear the system. For the individual on the spectrum this may take far longer; the difficulties processing what has happened mean that instead of calming down, the panic rises as they try to work out what has happened. They want to understand; they can't; they become frustrated and angry and this feeling can last minutes, or hours, or the whole day. Adrenaline surges through the system throughout the day and its effects may last for days, leaving the person in a constant state of fear.

Another aspect of the high levels of fear that the child feels is that memories of that event will trigger the same reaction in the future, when placed in a similar situation or with the same group of people. All those intense emotions will come pouring back and send them into a blind panic. Try to imagine what it must be like trying to function while experiencing such an onslaught on the senses and emotions.

They will be unable to recognize that they are in a dangerous situation until they are actually in it. Or they may never see it... You will have to lay down a few rules, which they can use when they get older, to tell them that they must not do certain things and explain what might happen if they do.

Lack of inhibition

fMRI research has revealed that underconnectivity between various areas in the brains of people with autism (and ADHD) leads to a lack of inhibition and impulse control. This leads to:

- difficulties in Executive Function (organization skills);
- narrow interests;

- the need for rigid routine;
- language processing (literal interpretation);
- inappropriate behaviour.

It has also been linked to the lack of Theory of Mind (the ability to predict what another person is thinking or intends to do).

The effect of a disordered inhibitory system has implications for learning that are not immediately obvious. Research into language and metaphor comprehension in individuals with autism found that the reader must suppress knowledge of one object that is totally irrelevant to the analogy. The example was 'Lawyers are sharks'. The intended analogy was that they are aggressive and ferocious, not that they have fins and sharp teeth (Gernsbacher and Robertson, 1999).

NT children will have learned from experience and be able to act intuitively, but the child with autism has to consciously work through the complicated process involved in making the right choice:

1 Assess the situation: *which they have difficulty 'reading'.*
2 Choose what to do next: *which they may perceive as a totally new experience and have not a clue what to do, so do the first thing that pops into their mind.*
3 Assess their choice of action or words: *by this time they are likely to be stressed.*
4 Recognize that there might be a problem with what they are about to do or say: *not if they are now panicking.*
5 Make a decision based upon what they think might be the consequence of their actions: *unlikely they will be able to process this far.*
6 Choose what to do next to adapt their behaviour or language: *totally unable to do this.*
7 Then do it: *Too late!*

Pupils with AS often 'challenge' those people around them due to a lack of inhibition. These actions are due to poor neural connections, which fail to suppress 'inappropriate behaviour' until they are specifically taught the hidden social codes.

Children with AS have no natural respect for authority. If you are a teacher you are expected to know your subject. If you make an error they will tell you, reasoning that it's not logical to want to make a mistake or leave it uncorrected. If you ask a question, they will give you an honest answer. Be careful about what you ask and the way you word a question. Social situations can be tricky because the individual will not adhere to the unwritten rules and will say exactly what they think, regardless of the fact that they may be perceived as disrespectful, rude, or even offensive.

Never lie to a pupil with AS. They will not understand the motivation behind it, and may take it as an attempt to humiliate them and never forgive you. Remember, we are the adults and the pupil with AS has no intention of being rude or disrespectful, they are just saying it how it is.

Executive Function – organization skills

The ability to plan and carry out complex cognitive tasks – to organize oneself – is also governed by complex brain processes. Called Executive Function, in autism this ability is interfered with by dysfunction in the frontal lobes of the brain. EF deficit includes a poor working memory, inattention, and difficulties initiating, sustaining and inhibiting actions.

It is important to understand that the neurobiological differences impact on the behaviour of the individual with AS. It is not a choice, and it should inform us as to how we manage the pupil in school.

Imagine:

- What it is like to be frightened every day of your life because your brain cannot predict what is going to happen next.
- Trying to concentrate while your body is being tortured.
- Living in a world surrounded by beings you cannot understand: it feels as if you have come from a different planet.

3 Autism and Asperger Syndrome – a brief history

No-one really knows what causes autism. It is not a modern phenomenon. There are the old tales of changeling children, stolen by the faeries and replaced with an identical child who screams and behaves 'badly'. Professor Uta Frith, a psychologist and world authority on ASCs, recounts in her book, *Autism: Explaining the Enigma*, a number of stories of people who display autistic behaviour. One example is Brother Juniper.

Brother Juniper, who lived in twelfth-century Italy, went to visit a sick brother in the hospital. When asked if there was anything he could do for him, the sick brother told Brother Juniper he'd love to have a pig's foot to eat. Brother Juniper went into the forest with a knife from the kitchens and cut off the foot of a live pig and carefully prepared a meal, which the sick brother enjoyed enormously. The owner of the maimed pig complained to the Franciscans but Brother Juniper could not comprehend what he had done wrong.

He was also in the habit of giving people anything they needed, including his clothes. He was told not to do that anymore. However, the next time he met a beggar Brother Juniper told him that he could not give him his clothes but if the beggar took his habit off him he would not stop him.

Frith also describes the Holy or Blessed Fools of Russia, whom she believes may have been autistic. They had no social awareness. Some roamed around naked, having a lack of sensitivity to pain, cold or hunger. They are reported as performing bizarre, ritualistic behaviour; Pelagija Serebrenikova, for example, collected stones and bricks and placed them beside a flooded pit. She threw them into the water. When they had all gone she waded into the pit and threw them out onto the side and repeated the exercise for years.

Some of these holy fools were mute; others ranted in the streets and talked gibberish, parroted people or spoke inappropriately. Treated with tolerance because of their isolation and physical hardship, they were considered touched by God and their bizarre behaviour was given significance in legends as lessons in life. They addressed Tsars and religious leaders without fear. Blessed Basil, fool for Christ, who robbed from the rich to feed the poor, is probably the most famous holy fool. He was canonized despite his criticism of Ivan the Terrible, whom he confronted about his brutality.

Today the most famous people with autism are: Dr Temple Grandin, professor of animal science, inventor, author and lecturer in autism education; Stephen Wiltshire, artist; and Carly Fleischmann, author, non-verbal autistic, who started her degree, age 18, at the University of Toronto in 2013.

Asperger Syndrome is different from classic autism (Kanner Syndrome) and is the most common form of autism found in mainstream schools. It is named after Hans Asperger (pronounced with a hard g), an Austrian psychiatrist who wrote a paper in 1944 about his observations of a group of children. While of average or high intelligence, they displayed untypical behaviour. They used formal and unconventional language; had poor social skills; lacked empathy for their peers; had an all-absorbing interest that dominated conversation;

displayed idiosyncratic behaviour; and were physically awkward. Lorna Wing, a British psychiatrist, coined the name in a 1981 paper in which she described Asperger's symptoms in a group of children she was studying.

In 1989 Christopher Gillberg, Professor of Child and Adolescent Psychiatry at Gothenburg University, Sweden, published the first set of criteria for Asperger Syndrome. It is considered to be the closest to Asperger's original description of the condition.

Little was known about Asperger's work in the English-speaking world until 1991, when Uta Frith translated Gillberg's paper into English from German.

In 1992 Asperger Syndrome was included in the World Health Organization's International Classification of Diseases (ICD-10) and in 1994 it was added to the American Psychiatric Association's (APA) *Diagnostic and Statistical Manual of Mental Disorders* (DSM-IV). These publications are the most popular references for a diagnosis.

Asperger Syndrome, as a separate condition, has been removed from DSM-5, published in May 2013. It has been replaced by the umbrella term Autistic Spectrum Disorder, with three levels of severity in order to provide a more precise diagnosis. However, recent fMRI (brain scan) research suggests that Asperger Syndrome is measurably different from autism.

It is generally agreed that AS is genetic and that the autistic brain begins to form mid-term during pregnancy, although brain damage caused by accidents, for example, can result in the person developing autistic characteristics. The greater prevalence of AS today can be explained by better diagnosis, larger populations and higher survival rates among children. The environment we live in today is not very autism friendly and their difficulties are more obvious. Education is a social activity because we expect children to work in pairs or groups and to discuss ideas and share opinions. A person with AS has social difficulties rooted in language impairment and rigid behaviour and will, therefore, stand out more in the modern classroom. Children with AS have fewer problems with speaking, although they can be quite literal in their interpretation of language, and are of average, or above average, intelligence.

Autism spectrum conditions cannot be 'cured' with medical intervention, although there are a number of therapies, including diet, which may lessen the effects of the conditions. It is a disorder of the brain, not a mental illness, although other illnesses, like depression, learning disorders such as dyslexia, motor difficulties such as hypermobility and dyspraxia, and Attention Deficit Hyperactivity Disorder (ADHD) may also co-exist.

The difference between autism and Asperger Syndrome is simply that in autism there is a developmental delay that is absent in AS. Indeed, children with AS may appear to be ahead of their peers in many areas such as language and reading. Children with AS can appear to be academically ahead of their peers in primary school; however, a word of caution, the difficulties experienced by a child with AS or HFA are very complex and very real. Unfortunately, it is largely a hidden disability and these children may need their support increased as they progress through school and their differences emerge, especially in those areas that require social interaction either in the learning environment or at play time.

Famous people diagnosed with Asperger Syndrome today include Paddy Considine, actor; Pip Brown aka Ladyhawke, singer songwriter; Daniel Tammet, savant, author, mathematician, multi-linguist; Gary McKinnon, computer hacker; and Clay Marzo, professional surfer.

The diagnosis journey

Children can be diagnosed with autism from the age of 18 months using ChAT (Checklist for Autism in Toddlers). If a parent or carer is concerned about the development of their child they will usually fill in a short questionnaire with their primary healthcare worker at the 18-month developmental check-up. It is the first step to obtaining a diagnosis. Its purpose is to identify children who are at risk of social-communication disorders.

Many children with HFA and Asperger Syndrome are diagnosed between the ages of 5 and 9. This is because there is no apparent developmental delay such as might have prompted an earlier diagnosis for other disorders. Others may only be recognized once they are in secondary school.

Some children may be missed altogether and grow up to be adults describing themselves as introverts or shy; indulging in life-long hobbies; becoming scientific researchers and leading lights in their careers. Others may suffer from loneliness, depression and isolation, unable to connect with their peers and regarded as odd and unsociable. Some develop strategies to be able to manage themselves and, while they may acknowledge that they have autistic traits, are never recognized as being on the spectrum.

Once the possibility of autism has been established, the parents can request their GP to refer them to be diagnosed for an ASC. One of the first things to be assessed is the child's hearing and sight, followed by an in-depth, multi-agency diagnostic process.

Initially a very detailed family history is taken by a medical professional trained in ASCs, usually in the form of an Autism Diagnostic Interview (ADI-R) or the Diagnostic Interview for Social and Communication Disorders (DISCO). This is followed by an Autism Diagnostic Observation Schedule (ADOS), where an educational psychologist observes the child over several hours in school or nursery; they will then go on to do a cognitive assessment (IQ test) appropriate to the child's age, such as the Wechsler Intelligence Scale (WISC). A speech and language therapist will do a communication assessment, because a communication deficit is one of the fundamental markers for a child with an ASC.

There are also other issues to be considered because other conditions often co-exist alongside autism. So the child will be assessed for ADHD, Sensory Processing Disorder and hypermobility or dyspraxia, and chromosomal analysis for Fragile X will also be investigated. Therefore there may be speech and language therapists assessing use of language; educational psychologists observing the child in school; physiotherapists conducting physical assessments; and neurological consultants doing EEGs and or MRIs. After which the professionals will get together to make a diagnosis – or not.

Contrary to popular belief, getting a diagnosis of autism is a complicated process. Some parents report that it can take anything up to seven years or longer.

The condition is very complex and may also co-exist with other conditions, for example, ADHD, Tourette's, Pathological Demand Avoidance (PDA), Irritable Bowel Syndrome, dyspraxia and hypermobility, which are all considered to be part of an ASC but not necessarily present in all children with an ASC. Autism is a heterogeneous condition in that there is not a single characteristic shared by everyone with an ASC. It is a complex brain disorder that can be affected by the environment because children with an ASC have to be taught everything – they do not naturally pick up social skills through intuition or observation.

Signs of Autism Spectrum Condition in young children

Very often it is teachers or teaching assistants in mainstream schools, who identify that there is a problem with the young child's development and a need to have a child assessed for ASCs. See below for a weblink to NICE's Quick Reference Guide to *Autism: Recognition, referral and diagnosis of children and young people on the autism spectrum*, to assess whether you should bring your concern regarding the child's behaviour to the attention of the SENCo and the child's parents.

Be aware of the delicacy of the situation. Although more people have heard of autism, some parents may be completely ignorant of the condition and require sensitive handling. Therefore, be prepared for a range of reactions and have helpful information to hand, such as may be found on the NAS website. You will need to justify your concerns and help them with the first step to diagnosis, should they wish to pursue it.

Further reading

Attwood, T. (2006). *The Complete Guide to Asperger Syndrome.* London: Jessica Kingsley Publishers.
Frith, U. (2003). *Autism: Explaining the Enigma.* 2nd edition. Malden, MA, and Oxford: Wiley-Blackwell.

Websites

http://www.autism.org.uk/about-autism/autism-and-asperger-syndrome-an-introduction.asp
   National Autistic Society (national charity), providing information, strategies and links to other useful sites.
'Autism – Recognition, referral and diagnosis of children and young people on the autism spectrum' at http://guidance.nice.org.uk/CG128/QuickRefGuide/pdf/English.
'Inclusion Development Programme: Supporting pupils on the autism spectrum – an interactive resource for headteachers, leadership teams, teachers, teaching assistants and the ITT audience.' http://www.idponline.org.uk/psautism/launch.html.

4   Girls with Asperger Syndrome

Statistically, only 1 in 4 people diagnosed with AS are female. There is growing concern that girls are being overlooked and that the figure is nearer 1 in 2. Females with AS seem to be better able to mask the condition by observing and copying their peers and, therefore, appear to be more socially adept, but often you will find that they have few friends and tend to focus on one person at a time.

Girls have better imaginations than boys and often have a 'fantasy' life and invisible friends. Interests may be cloaked in typical female behaviour, but they are more intensely involved or appear to be unconventional. They may be totally uninterested in their appearance and even prefer to dress like a tomboy, or they may be very interested in fashion and develop their own unique style. Most girls with AS choose not to draw attention to themselves; they have learned that this world doesn't operate the way they see it so they fall silent and observe. Pay attention to the girls who have difficulties and are very quiet in lessons. Are they copying their peers? How do they respond if you give them an ambiguous instruction? Are they often to be found by themselves in the playground or on the very outside of a group of their peers?

Currently, the female pupil diagnosed with AS may appear to be more extreme because she fits into the male model of an individual with AS. It has now been recognized that many females with AS do not fit into the diagnostic criteria of AS, which are heavily biased towards the behaviour of boys. There is a movement to develop a range of criteria appropriate to the diagnosis of girls with AS in the future.

There is a critical need in this area, not least to address the mental health issues associated with teenagers and women on the spectrum, particularly among those who are not yet diagnosed. A growing body of autobiographical literature written by women who were diagnosed later in life reveals that many suffer from depression, anxiety, eating disorders, self-harm and behavioural problems and show a lack of social skills especially in group situations, while able to sustain a close friendship with one other person at a time, and this person may change frequently.

Further reading

Marshall, T. A. (2014). *I am AspienGirl*. http://www.aspiengirl.com/english.

Riley-Hall, E. (2012). *Parenting Girls on the Autism Spectrum: overcoming the challenges and celebrating the gifts*. London: Jessica Kingsley Publishers.

Sainsbury, C. (2003). *Martian in the Playground: understanding the schoolchild with Asperger's syndrome*. London: Sage Publications Inc.

Simone, R. (2010). *Aspergirls: empowering females with Asperger syndrome*. London: Jessica Kingsley Publishers.

5   Parents are a valuable resource – use them

The mother knows the child better than anyone else. If the child is seven years old, that is the amount of time it takes to be awarded a PhD, so a mother of a seven-year-old child has an honorary PhD in the study of that child. I know to listen to mother's knowledge and advice. She will provide continuity and experience for the child's lifetime.

Tony Attwood

Writing this chapter, as a parent of a child with Asperger Syndrome, I would like to say that we really appreciate professionals who take the time to talk to us and learn about AS, to inform themselves as to the best way to support our children.

With all the challenges that face our children and the lack of understanding of autism in mainstream education, we have high levels of anxiety too. All we ask is that you remember Every Child Matters and our children need you to understand what it means to have autism and how that impacts on their daily lives.

Also consider how having a child on the spectrum affects our daily lives too, as we organize our days to support our children, helping them to feel safe and competent; wanting them to be valued and accepted for who they are. They are just children. Please, work with us to help our children.

Dear SENCo,

I would like to offer you the opportunity to engage with me regarding (my child), who has been diagnosed with an Autism Spectrum Condition (ASC). Autism is a heterogeneous condition and I am uniquely placed to offer you information pertinent to (my child) and how we might best enable him/her to thrive under your care and fulfil his/her academic potential.

Having a diagnosis of an ASC means that (my child) has a lifelong, pervasive developmental disorder that affects the physiology of the brain, resulting in cognitive processing difficulties and impairments in language, sensory processing and social communication. My child has certain rigid behaviours, a need for routine and is hyper or hypo sensitive to certain sensory input. His/her behaviour is not a choice but a direct result of different wiring in the brain.

A hidden disability, autism means that (my child) may appear, on the surface, to be high functioning when, in reality, surviving the school environment, decoding instructions, meeting the education demands and negotiating social interactions in myriad situations requires a huge effort. This places huge stresses upon (my child) as s/he attempts to meet the expectations of teachers, teaching assistants and peers in circumstances that are often confusing, due to a lack of understanding of what s/he is supposed to do. This can result in overload or burn out leading to shut-down or meltdown, which is distressing for all concerned.

I can be a valuable resource and help you to understand the impact autism has upon my child and effective strategies to support him/her in your school. I would like to meet with you, as soon as possible, to discuss assessment of his/her needs and put together a range of strategies for the mutual benefit of (my child) and the school.

Sincerely…

A word in your ear

The histories of autistic families reveal clear evidence to suggest that AS is genetic. If a family has a child with AS, there is a high probability that one or both parents are on the spectrum too. This should inform your dealings with them. Far too often, we make judgements about mothers of children with AS, struggling to get the best support for their children:

> The mum with Executive Functioning difficulties that forgets appointments (seen as neglect), the mum with Aspergers who struggles with tone in voice patterns (perceived as aggressive), the mum with Sensory Processing Disorder, who is in pain from sensory stimuli and is pacing (seen as a threat).
>
> Monique Blakemore

From my own experience as both a TA and a parent, we are considered to be quite difficult to deal with. All we, as parents, want is to know that you are keeping our child safe, meeting their needs and enabling them to progress by building on their strengths.

Regular, twice-termly meetings with parents with autistic children, regardless of whether they have a statement of SEN, are important and can be mutually beneficial. Emails or telephone calls with good news are very encouraging. Don't just call us when something goes wrong. Work done in school may be supplemented at home in ways more appropriate to the child, for example a trip to a museum or even a video game on a subject, which the school cannot provide.

Introducing parents with Asperkids to each other can often lead to friendships outside school for the whole family. The pupils benefit by having more opportunities to develop their social skills and form meaningful relationships with their peers. The parents get support from other adults, who understand better than anyone else what they are going through.

The Comms Book

A Comms Book is an exercise book in which TAs, teachers and parents relay information about how the pupil is managing their day in school and at home during term time. For example, a parent or carer may wish to communicate that the pupil has had a difficult start to the morning, having had a meltdown due to a row with a sibling; or the teacher tell the parents that their child worked well in a lesson, in a group, or that the pupil forgot their pencil case.

It should be read by the teacher/TA every day and at each hand-over. You will gain useful information about how the pupil is managing their day and how they are likely to perform in their lessons, or whether further adjustments need to be made.

Use the Comms Book to relay the following information:

- Progress in class: do not underestimate the value of praise, but it must be earned or the pupil will not trust you in future.
- Difficulties in lessons/subjects.
- Interaction with peers.
- Information about forthcoming changes to routines or staff, so that parents can prepare the pupil beforehand.
- School trips, activities, clubs and after school events – the pupil is unlikely to remember to pass on any notices of events to parents, so staple these into the Comms Book!
- Questions to the other party if clarification is needed.
- Comments on health.
- Likes or dislikes.

The Comms Book can be used to apply consistency of approach across the curriculum during the school day, as school staff and parents share with each other what works effectively to support the pupil, help them to feel secure and keep them calm.

Families with a child with AS have higher levels of stress and anxiety than those with other SENs and are more likely to require support. Using a Comms Book to let them know how their child has managed the day will go a long way to reassure them that you are looking after their vulnerable child and monitoring any changes in behaviour. The pupil is unlikely to disclose what happened during the school day to their parents or carers until days, months or years after the actual event, due to the way the autistic brain processes information.

BE HONEST! We can best support our children in mainstream education if you tell us the truth.

The Comms Book is *not* a Complaints Book. Always try and find something positive to say – negative comments are not seen as constructive criticism by pupils with AS and can have a devastating effect on self-esteem. Take care how you express anything negative. If the pupil has access to the Comms Book and can read it, they may take it personally and believe that you don't like them, and this will make supporting the pupil difficult. The best approach is to suggest an alternative way of managing the situation: Tom had difficulty queuing for his lunch today and pushed another pupil out of the way. He should be encouraged to show his pass and say 'excuse me' to the pupils he is overtaking.

Let us help you help our children! You are the education experts, we are the experts in our children. We need to work together and exchange strategies.

Part Two

6 Be prepared! Transition into primary school

In primary school you are going to work with children who already have a diagnosis of autism and those who have yet to be diagnosed. When receiving a child with a diagnosis, practical preparation for transition should start at the beginning of the summer term at the very latest, before September entry. This is vital for the child with AS, who may struggle to make sense of the world they live in. The unexpected is terrifying and the source of great anxiety and stress. The parent will also be anxious because they know their child is different from his or her peers and very vulnerable because their behaviour is often misinterpreted by adults, who do not understand the impact having AS has on the child.

A different environment, like a school, with lots of strange noises, smells, sights, textures – for example, bright lights, garish colours, strange adults and large rooms full of other children – is utterly petrifying. And not just for a few seconds or minutes – anxiety can persist for the whole of the school day. For many children it will be the first time that they enter into the world of their peers. A change in routine, meeting strangers in an alien environment that assaults their senses, and a feeling of helplessness, not being able to control what is happening, may raise anxiety levels to a degree where their behaviour will be out of their control.

The child with an ASC will react in very different ways. Young children are naturally egocentric and curious. The child with autism may appear totally self-absorbed in a world of their own, separate from their surroundings, always on the periphery of whatever is going on, gazing out of the window or fixated on something you can't see. They may block out what is going on around them to manage the new experience, focusing on a single detail that claims their attention for a long time.

They may cling to their mother, utterly distraught and demanding to go home, day after day after day. Then, when the parent has left, they will instantly stop crying and get on with it as best they can until their parent returns, and then they will start crying again. In these circumstances, it is worth remembering that the child's lack of social imagination means that they do not 'know' that their parent will be there to collect them at the end of the day, no matter how many times they leave to meet them in the playground at the end of school. It is not generally a sign of Attachment Disorder, which is a very serious mental illness.

Top Tip

Put a photo in the child's daily timetable of Mum, Dad, Gran… waiting in the playground to meet the child at the end of that day.

Another child with AS may pursue a sensation or experience with little awareness of what is going on around them and what you want them to do. They may be seeking a sensation or favourite activity with a singlemindedness that will make it difficult for you to divert their attention.

They are likely to have no off switch because they act on impulse, which they will be unable to regulate, and you may find some of the behaviour difficult to manage unless you work with their strengths and interests and feed their sensory needs.

Most children with AS are resistant to change because they are anxious and scared of the unknown; they want to do well but don't know what is expected of them. They cannot predict what's going to happen next and they may lack cognitive empathy and have difficulty imagining what you are thinking. Because you are in the same space at the same time, sharing the same experiences, they imagine you are thinking exactly the same things that they are.

To help prepare for September, learn as much as you can about individual children from their parents and their nursery. They are all different and their condition will affect them in different ways.

The SENCo should assign at least two TAs to the pupil, so that if one is off there will be some continuity of care with the other TA, who is familiar to the pupil. To ensure that this is in place, write it into the EHCP.

Strategies

Research

Use the Transition Questionnaire to record information:

- Consult the parents or carers – they know their child better than anyone. If the child doesn't go to nursery, make an appointment to visit them at home.
- Send the Transition Questionnaire to the nursery or visit the nursery yourself.
- Read the reports from medical professionals involved in their diagnosis: psychologists, paediatricians, speech and language therapists, occupational therapists, physiotherapists, counsellors: everyone! And build up a *positive* profile.
- Use the Transition Questionnaire (Table 6.1) to record all the relevant information from all your sources to create an ASC Passport for the child.

Table 6.1 Transition Questionnaire

Name:	
DoB:	
Nursery School:	
Date:	
Home Communication Preferences: regular meetings, comms book, telephone, email, recording device…?	
Sensory Issues?	
Toilet	
Other causes of distress: teasing, criticism, reprimanding…	
Tell Signs of Distress	
Alert System – Smileys, 5 point scale, traffic lights	
Calming Strategies, Stims	
Use of Social Stories or Comic Conversations in nursery or at home	
Special Interests	
Timetable – visual, colour coded, written	
Movement between different locations	
Communication	
Learning Style – visual, aural, kinaesthetic	
Concentration Level	
Strengths	
Weaknesses	
Flexibility	
Social Skills	

Pupil Passport

Ask the pupil's parents to put together a passport to introduce you to their child, using Template 6.1. With all the information gathered, write a Pupil Passport for every member of staff who will be in contact with them on a regular basis. Include receptionists, administration staff, dinner ladies, librarians, technicians, caretakers and groundsmen, using Template 6.2. The Pupil Passport should be available to *everyone* before the pupil arrives.

A poster in the staffroom with photographs of *all* pupils with an ASC will help the staff who don't teach them to recognize them around the school and in the playground. Adding their particular interest will also help staff to communicate with them in a meaningful way. If the pupil needs help calming down, ask a question about their special interest.

If there is a problem with the pupil's preference to play alone or with anti-social behaviour, the teacher will know that this is most likely a result of their ASC rather than any malicious intent. If the pupil is on the periphery of other pupils messing around and he reacts badly to being shouted at, it will be invaluable to the member of staff on duty to know why.

Print the Pupil Passport on brightly coloured paper and distribute it to: teachers, support staff, senior management team, on call team, cover supervisors and supply teachers as necessary. It should be treated as Confidential Information.

Keep the writing to a minimum: use key words. Staff need to be able to access the information quickly, in some cases just before the start of a lesson.

Include the following information:

- **Name**: Form, Form Tutor, passport size photograph.
- **Strengths:** Lego building, dinosaurs, Romans.
- **Support strategies and Top Tips:** Unambiguous language, visual aids, colour coding, name first, do not force eye contact.
- **Triggers or Stressors:** Shouting, lights, teasing.
- **Calming Strategies:** Stim – stroking velvet in pocket, time out, carrying heavy books.
- **Alert**: Phobias – spiders, wasps, the colour orange; writing can also be a phobia because of need to produce a 'perfect' piece of work.

Hello!

Insert photo here

My name is ....

I will be in your class in ....

I worry and get anxious when ....

....

....

....

....

You can help me by ....

....

....

....

Things that upset me ....

....

....

....

....

....

....

Things that calm me ....

....

....

....

Meet my family

Here is ....

....

....

....

7   2

My pet/s

I have a .... called ....

I like ....

I don't like ....

My favourite activities are ....

My favourite toys are ....

Template 6.2 – Change to Pupil Passport

Affix
'passport' photo
here

Name:..

Form:..

Tutor:..

Room:..

My Strengths: ....

....

....

Support Strategies: ....

....

....

....

....

Triggers or Stressors: ....

....

....

Calming Strategies: ....

....

....

....

....

Name of Key Staff: ....

Welcome pack

Send this to the parents of the prospective pupil in the summer term so that they can prepare their child for school in September.

Each topic for the pupil should be supported with visual references. Include:

- A First Day in School Programme of Events; this will help prepare the pupils for a special assembly or any deviation from the normal timetable.
- A colour-coded, visual timetable for a normal day to put up at home. Match the colour on the timetable to the colour of their books for that subject.
- Assembly Days.
- School Rules.
- What will happen if… the child is injured, bullied or property is lost.
- Uniform and PE kit – photographs.

School visits

- Invite the pupil to visit the school several times with a parent or carer. The first visit should be when the school is quiet and all the children have gone home.
- The invitation should be made with lots of visual references, which the parent or carer can go through with their child before the visit to your school. Use as few words as possible to put your message across. See the template below. I have used the first person to help the child visualize themselves visiting the school.
- The pupil's key TA should meet and guide the child on all their visits.

1

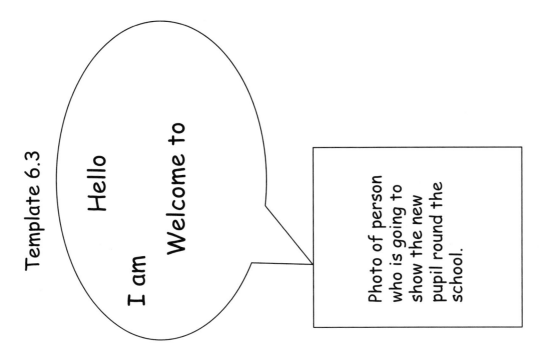

Hello

I am

Welcome to

Photo of person who is going to show the new pupil round the school.

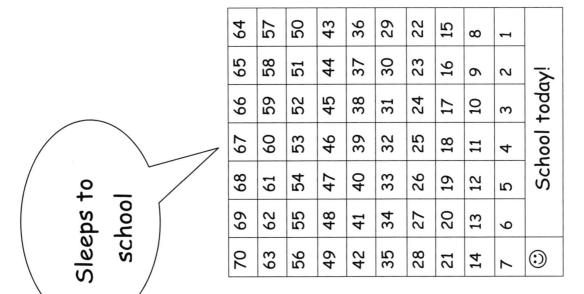

Sleeps to school

70	69	68	67	66	65	64		
63	62	61	60	59	58	57		
56	55	54	53	52	51	50		
49	48	47	46	45	44	43		
42	41	40	39	38	37	36		
35	34	33	32	31	30	29		
28	27	26	25	24	23	22		
21	20	19	18	17	16	15		
14	13	12	11	10	9	8		
7	6	5	4	3	2	1		
☺				School today!				

8

Playground

Photo of person who is going to show the new pupil round the school.

School

Photo of person who is going to show the new pupil round the school.

Uniform

PE Kit

Everyday uniform

Classroom

Have them bring a camera to record the visit. Photograph the pupil in places of their interest. This will help them visualize themselves in these new surroundings. When they return to their nursery or home they can then make a booklet and familiarize themselves with their new school during the summer holidays. See the template below, 'Things I will do in my school'. The last photo, the pupil in uniform, should be taken by the parent ready for their first day at school and the pupil should bring in the booklets (6.3, 6.4 and 6.5) to help them recognize relevant places and people after the long holiday.

Things I will do in my school!

┌─────────────────────────┐
│   │
│   │
│   Picture of school   │
│   │
│   │
└─────────────────────────┘

I am ready to go to school!

┌─────────────────────────┐
│   │
│   │
│   Photo of   │
│   pupil in school   │
│   uniform   │
│   │
│   │
└─────────────────────────┘

8 1

I eat my lunch in the ....

```
┌─────────────────────────────┐
│                             │
│                             │
│                             │
│     Photo of dining area    │
│                             │
│                             │
│                             │
└─────────────────────────────┘
```

After lunch I will play in the playground with my friends.

```
┌─────────────────────────────┐
│                             │
│                             │
│                             │
│  Photo of Teacher in classroom │
│                             │
│                             │
│                             │
└─────────────────────────────┘
```

I meet my teacher in my classroom.

My teacher is ....

My class is ....

At break I will play in the playground with my friends.

Playground with children playing.

We will play

I will go with the class to Assembly in the Hall.

Hall at Assembly

I will sit ....

....

....

The end of Assembly we go back to class.

5

4

In my classroom is

＿＿＿＿＿

＿＿＿＿＿

＿＿＿＿＿

＿＿＿＿＿

I will do PE outside.

And I will do PE inside.

Key members of staff

- Give the pupil photographs of key staff they will see during the school day, in the places they work: the Principal in assembly, admin staff and receptionists in their offices, dinner ladies and the school caretaker doing their jobs, the librarian, head of year, SENCo, TAs and form tutor in the classroom. See the template below, 'People who will help me at school'.
- Make a card game, see below, to help familiarize the pupil with the members of staff with whom they will have regular contact.

People who
help me at school

Group Photo

the caretaker

....
looks after the school buildings.
8

1

the receptionist

meets people when they come to school.

7

my teacher

teaches me.

2

my buddy

the dinner ladies

helps me at break times.

help me at lunchtime.

4

5

the classroom helper/s

helps me with my work in lessons.

3

the head teacher

is in charge of the school.

6

Card games

A fun way to help familiarize the child with the school and staff, **Happy School Days** is a card game adapted from Happy Families and Pairs to introduce the pupil to staff in schools, their job and locations.

Photographs:

- passport photo of key staff;
- place of work: office, kitchen, canteen, reception, classroom, sports field...
- staff *doing* their job;
- the tools of the job.

Photographs should be the size of a playing card. Fix photographs onto the same coloured card, using different colours to differentiate the type of picture: for example, people – blue; place – green; job – pink; tools – yellow; laminate and cut each photo into individual cards to make a pack.

Give the pack of cards to the parent to play the game throughout the holiday before starting school in September.

Familiarization can be developed further after term starts with the following games.

Where are they?

Draw a simple map of the school, photocopy onto A3 paper and laminate. Differentiate to meet the needs of the pupil by:

- Putting a picture of the staff member in their 'space' (if the child has a problem with facial recognition to match up to a loose card of the person).
- Inserting a symbol of the room's use, if it is specific: books – library; knife and fork – canteen; football – sports field; piano – music area... be careful to explain multiple use – timeline showing hall being used for assembly then gym later in the day. They don't have to be able to read it, colour code the time block to match their colour coded subject timetable.
- Putting a picture of the child in their classroom in uniform, library with a book, in the gym in their PE kit, in the music room with an instrument...

Make a set of cards of the people the pupil will come into contact with: TA, teacher, playtime supervisor, dinner lady, receptionist, principal... in the same backing colour.

Make a set of cards of the different activities the pupil will do in different places: PE – a football; assembly – photo of the event; lunch – knife and fork; playground – play activities; fire 'station', and anything else appropriate to your school.

Happy school days – Rules for home

The object of the game is to collect 2/3/4 cards, building it up over a period of weeks or months, as long as it takes:

- Person + Job
- Person + Place
- Person + Tools
- Person + Job + Place
- Person + Job + Place + Tools.

Lay the cards on the floor face up and match the pairs.

When your child is confident as to who does what, or where they can find each person, or all three, turn them over to hide the face of the cards and play the game of finding and matching.

- Deal a card to the child one at a time.
- Direct, 'Mrs Smith – classroom,' or 'Put Mrs Smith in her classroom', or 'Mrs Smith is…?' The player could also be encouraged to say where.
- For every correct answer give a token and reward, as appropriate.
- Start with a minimum of two members of staff – key TA and teacher. Play the game to teach the child where s/he can find them; introduce different times of the school day; then add more staff whom the child meets: the dinner lady and receptionist, for example.
- For every correct answer give a token and reward as appropriate.

Taster lessons

- During the summer term, invite the pupil to attend a lesson in their favourite topic.
- Use this opportunity to observe and record how the child reacts in lessons with support from their TA or parent.
- On another visit you could work with the pupil and begin to build a good working relationship.
- Observe their social skills.

Inset Day presentation

- SENCo should introduce the whole staff to the pupils with ASCs.
- Presentation should include a photo of the pupils with a run-through of their AS Passport.
- *All* staff should take note. They may not teach them but they may encounter the pupils elsewhere. Knowing he or she has AS may make a world of difference to the way they handle a situation and the pupil.

First day at school

- The key TA, who escorted the pupil during the summer term visits, should be assigned to work with the pupil, for the first week at the very least.

- Meet the pupil as you did during the visits to the school during the summer term. The same experience will help to settle them.
- Go over the school day.
- Remind the pupil that they will be collected at the end of the day by their parent or carer.
- It may be worth considering a staggered introduction into school: Week 1 and 2 mornings only; Week 3 and 4 mornings and lunchtime; Weeks 5 and 6 all day.

Build a relationship

Lastly and probably most importantly:

- Meet the pupil every morning to take them through their day and sit down and talk to them to get to know them. This will help you build a relationship of trust.
- Find out what frightens them in school that is likely to cause stress.
- Keep up to date with what they do like and what may calm them down.
- This information will help you develop bespoke strategies and options to enable them to help themselves: exit cards, mood meter, haven – they may prefer the library or a walk outside.

A good relationship with the pupil is important but be aware that you may become the only person that the child trusts and therefore becomes totally dependent upon while in school. There is a risk that this will impact on the pupil's ability to function without their key worker, so it is probably wise to have at least two learning support/teaching assistants.

Top Tip

Involve *everyone* in the school in autism awareness training. The pupil needs people who understand their difficulties anywhere, at any time.

7 Sensory overload – creating an autism-friendly environment

People with ASCs perceive the world and relate to it very differently from NTs, making them act differently too. This altered perspective is caused by the brain being wired in a way that makes them hypersensitive or hyposensitive to aspects of their environment. Sensory overload and the resultant chemical imbalance is often the key to negative emotional and behavioural responses due to stress and fear.

> The sensory overload caused by bright lights, fluorescent lights, colours and patterns makes the body react as if being attacked or bombarded, resulting in such physical symptoms as headaches, anxiety, panic attacks or aggression.
>
> Donna Williams

Assess the classroom, gym, hall… from the perspective of a young child on the autism spectrum, as Donna Williams does in her 1998 book, *Autism and Sensing: the unlost instinct*. What you perceive as a bright, colourful, noisy, busy, stimulating scene could be sensory hell for that child. Consider the behaviour in the classroom environment in this light and you may see it in a different way.

If a pupil with an ASC gets upset for no apparent reason, look carefully at how they are reacting to their environment. Is there a sensory reason for the behaviour? As the pupil gets older some of the sensory hypersensitivity can lessen, but the young child will not be able to manage their physical receptors and certain environments can be torturous for them.

Never touch a child with autism without giving a warning that you are going to do so. It is worth noting that the nerves that respond to a light or gentle touch are similar to those that detect pain. The light touch of another human, or even materials, can cause pain.

When you see the pupil tense, drop their head, put their hands over their ears, hug themselves, flap, pull their jumper over their heads, make a strange noise or scream and hide under the table or in a cupboard, and even become aggressive, remember that hypersensitivity to certain things can make them simply too much to bear for the child. It can trigger shutdown or meltdown. Have a *calm zone* in the classroom or use a Time Out card and remove them from the room to a safe place.

The seven sensory systems affected by autistic processing difficulties are: hearing, sight, touch, taste, smell, balance (vestibular), and space and movement (proprioception). Sensory stimuli disturbances are varied and particular to the individual. By making adjustments to the pupil's environment and allowances for the pupil's hypersensitivities, you will enhance their ability to learn by dampening the physical impact of sensory overload, thereby reducing anxiety and fear.

If you judge that the pupil is behaving in a certain way because they crave sensory input, giving them the appropriate stimulation (sensory snacks) through the school day to stabilise their senses will enable them to concentrate better during lessons.

When senses are disorganized, the ability to pay attention, learn and communicate are negatively affected. At this point – take time out.

Time out

Time out is a strategy that should be agreed before being put into use. It is not removal from the lesson as a punishment. Discuss the following with the older pupil beforehand:

- Time out is to support the pupil in times of sensory overload and distress.
- The Bombmeter is a tool to help you to gauge their stress level. Teach the pupil how to use the Bombmeter to help you gauge how they are feeling.
  - In Primary school it has 2, 3 and 5 levels.
  - In Reception and early years use the basic traffic light version: Green = I'm good; Amber = I don't know…; Red = Help!
  - You may only be able to use two colours at first: Red and Green.
  - From years 4 – 6 use the Bombmeter with five colours: blue, green, yellow, orange and red.
  - When you are first working with the pupil I advise you to remove them from the situation when in the orange zone. Later this may extend to the red zone. As you get to know your target pupil you may be able to distract them and talk them down but, in the meantime, take time out at 4.
- Take the pupil to a quiet area and distract them with a favourite activity to calm their senses.

Stimming

Stimming is self-stimulatory behaviour to self-regulate the senses. To stim (verb) means *indulging in self-stimulatory behaviours* or (noun) *a stimulatory behaviour*. Pupils with autism stim to distract themselves from something that is upsetting them, in an attempt to calm down. It is used to stimulate one sense in an effort to block out distractions from another sense when distressed or anxious. They also stim when happy or excited.

Stimming comes in many forms and is usually a repetitive movement of the body like rocking, tapping, bouncing, twirling, flapping of arms/hands, swaying from side to side and fiddling with or stroking an object. A pupil may stroke a piece of velvet, fiddle with a piece of string or squeeze a rubber ball to distract themselves from things you can't see or hear.

Other stims include noises, facial expressions, singing, humming, talking or babbling to oneself, clearing one's throat, nail (and finger) biting. Many of these behaviours are not tolerated socially in school so allow a more acceptable alternative using a sensory toy, a squeeze ball or everyday object, like a piece of string, that the pupil finds soothing.

NTs stim too, tapping their pens or feet and drumming fingers! It is an unconscious act. We don't stim to annoy people. It might be annoying but used as a calming tool, it should be allowed to continue until a more acceptable or discreet alternative is found to replace the behaviour.

Stimming enables the pupil to concentrate on their work. If you insist the pupil with AS stops stimming you will undermine their ability to do a task. They will have to use more of their reduced or depleted executive functioning skills to regulate their unconscious behaviour and, therefore, reduce their ability to perform well in the task.

This often results in burn out when the pupil returns home. They may seek the sensory input they have been deprived of at school and run around their home screaming or destroying things; they may curl up in a tight ball under a table or in a cupboard to try and desensitize their overloaded neural system. Parents will take their children to the playground after school to feed their sensory needs or get them home quickly and into the sensory room they will have made to meet their children's needs.

Many people see this as simply the inability of parents to control their children and not the school's problem. *But it is*. If the child goes home in this state they will be unable to do homework; they will have to take time to restore their neural system, which is exhausting, and the next day in school will be even harder for them to manage. So it would benefit the school to keep the child calm and able to learn in school and do the homework required.

Difficulties with the seven senses: Hyper-sensory

Sound

- Auditory disturbance is a common sensory issue for individuals with AS. They can often hear things we can't: the buzzing of lights, electricity, road noise and voices in another room are all distracting. Noise levels or pitch may be painful, including a person's voice. Potential difficulties may be found in: certain instruments in Music lessons; power tools and food mixers in Technology; the acoustics of the gym or main hall in PE or Dance.
- An acute sense of hearing means that the pupil can hear what is going on in the next room but cannot make sense of what the person sitting next to them is saying. They are oversensitive to certain sounds – a crisp packet scrunching to them is like the sound of nails on a chalkboard to an NT, and humming lights like a swarm of bees.
- There may also be difficulties with processing long-winded oral instructions because words become jumbled or lost and sentences take on a different meaning.
- The pupil may also talk very loudly or quietly, in a monotonous voice. They may have little awareness of the volume of their own voice.

Strategies

- Ear defenders are very effective, although discreet earplugs are more desirable.
- Give short, clear oral instructions.
- Lower your voice and speak quietly and calmly.
- Check instructions have been heard and understood by asking 'What does teacher want you to do?'. **Note:** repetition of instructions is not evidence of understanding.
- Write down instructions using as few words as possible with appropriate symbols or images.
- If the pupil shows signs of distress due to noise levels, remove them from the classroom to a quiet area until they are calm.
- Warn them beforehand when the bells or fire alarms are about to go off and take appropriate action.
- Alert the pupil through discreet signals if they are talking loudly.
- Make them aware of volume by recording a conversation to indicate the two levels – shouting and normal range.

Sight

- Visual disturbance may be caused by bright, flickering lights, which we don't see. Individuals with AS have reported their vision as being similar to over-exposure in taking a photograph and colours appearing to be brighter. The object they look at may appear distorted or even moving about. They may also be sensitive to a particular colour. Some pupils are distracted by displays of work on the wall or a cluttered desk and therefore are unable to concentrate on the task.
- Detailed focus processing is both a strength and weakness. Pupils may be unable to see the whole because they are captured by the detail. Attention to detail can be an advantage in certain tasks, providing they do not feel compelled to strive for perfection and destroy something they perceive as being sub-standard.
- When reading text they may have difficulty tracking lines of writing across paper. Hand to eye co-ordination may be clumsy because there may be problems with depth perception (see also Movement – Proprioception).
- Blurring may occur on the periphery of their vision or in the centre of their focus. Images may fracture and faces become distorted like Picasso paintings.

Strategies

- Switch off some or all of the lights. Install daylight bulbs.
- Seat the pupil with their back to the window.
- Allow them to wear tinted lenses or sunglasses indoors.
- Put coloured gels over text.
- Photocopy text onto beige or grey rather than white paper.
- Replace the colour of background in a display.
- Seat the pupil in a visually calm zone of the classroom facing a bare wall, or use a portable desk carrel (a three-sided, hinged screen).
- Remove the displays around the board or where the teacher stands at the front of the class.
- Keep the work area clear and clutter free.
- Use reading blinds to cover irrelevant text, diagrams or pictures in textbooks.
- Write on the board in different colours for each sentence in rotation to help differentiate between one sentence and the next.
- Use different colour inks to differentiate between subject matter.
- Teach the pupil how to cross out errors neatly, or use a pencil or a laptop.
- Be patient and allow time to process.
- The haven should be visually clear – avoid wall displays.

Touch

- Tactile disturbance can result in a light touch causing the pupil pain and a firm hold being felt as comforting. This may cause problems during transitions in a crowded corridor between lessons.
- Clothing may feel itchy or be painful to wear: wool feels like fibreglass, labels 'lacerate' the skin.
- Handling certain textures like paint and cooking ingredients may be intolerable. Water on the face can cause panic in swimming lessons.

Strategies

- Allow the pupil to move between areas a couple of minutes before everyone else.
- Plastic gloves can be useful – or cause more problems.
- Cut out clothing labels and try to be flexible in allowing alternatives to irritating clothing, if the uniform is painful.
- Do *not* attempt to desensitize the pupil. As they get older they may become desensitized naturally.
- *Do not remove stims,* because they help the pupil to regulate senses and emotions. If offensive, be imaginative and find a substitute. Put sensory stims into a box with a hole cut in the front, which can be unblocked to allow discreet access to them.

Taste and Smell

- **Gustatory and olfactory** disturbances can result in the pupil reacting negatively to certain situations and being a very picky eater, with a restricted diet. Strongly flavoured food may become too tasty after a while and the rest of the meal left on the plate. They have a keen sense of taste and will be able to detect the flavour of fish, used in animal feed, in chicken or pork, for example, which they may find repellant.
- Smells can be overwhelming for some pupils with AS. They may have difficulties in areas with strong smells: toilet, dining hall, sitting next to people they don't like the smell of. Perfume or deodorants can be overpowering, making the pupil nauseous. They may complain about a smell of burning, imperceptible to typical senses, from electric wires heating up.

Strategies

- Assign an MTA (Meal Times Assistant) to keep an eye on the pupil.
- Tolerance and flexibility are needed in the dining hall and when handling food.
- When eating, let them separate food out or they may be unable to eat it.
- A strong reaction to the smell and taste of food may be part of the way the condition impacts upon the pupil: find an alternative.
- If you are with a pupil who cannot stand the smell of perfume or deodorant, avoid wearing it that day.

Balance

- Vestibular system disturbance is where the inner ear receives misinformation about where we are in space from movement, speed and direction. Hypersensitivity in the vestibular system can result in feeling as though they are falling when standing up or sitting down. They can be clingy when moving around, or feel nauseous. They may experience fear of heights going up or down stairs. There may be difficulties sitting, or changing direction and speed, causing clumsiness. They are unlikely to ride a bike and will avoid anything that appears to be a bit risky.

Strategies

- Time out of the PE or Dance lesson to recover, if nauseous.
- Time in the sensory room on a gently swinging hammock (side to side swing).

Warning: Watch out for overstimulation. For example, too much spinning can lead to extreme motion sickness and the pupil may end up being unable to sit, stand or lie down without feeling nauseous. It is very similar to chronic car or seasickness.

Movement

The proprioception system – the way the brain perceives the body in space and controls our limbs or the movement system – may be disordered. Hypersensory proprioception means that the pupil will be super-aware of where their limbs are and be in some discomfort sitting still for any length of time.

Strategies

- Allow frequent movement breaks.
- Use move and sit cushions (PhysioRoom New Junior Air Stability Wobble Cushion from Amazon).
- Use Thera Band (available from Amazon) wrapped across the legs of a chair for the pupil to push against with their feet in lessons.

Difficulties with the seven senses: Hypo-sensory

The hyposensitive child is one who has difficulties processing information through their senses, resulting in under-sensitivity.

Sound

- Hyposensitive children love loud noises and sounds, enjoy loud music, and have difficulty regulating their volume of speech. They will seek situations that are noisy or make a lot of noise themselves.

Strategies

- Shouting, screaming, singing, animal noises and other sound effects, listening to loud music; songs like Old Macdonald's Farm, The Animals Went in Two by Two…
- Increase the volume of noise so that the pupil learns how to regulate sounds: for example, cat's meow, yowl, growl, roar! Which animals are quiet and which are loud?
- Playing musical instruments or listening to music. Often, playing music in the background can regulate the mood of the classroom. Alternatively, the pupil can listen to loud music on an iPod.

Vision

- Hyposensitive children may have difficulties tracking things with their eyes and seeing objects in sharp focus and will use their hands to support visual input. They may love bright colours and lights.

Strategies

- Glow wands, flashing lights, light spinners.
- Moving patterns – kaleidoscopes, windmills or whirly wheels.
- Glitter bottles.
- Water and oil bottles for two colours (Candy Color Set – Amazon.co.uk) and water; add transparencies with words relating to objects you can add to the mix (see http://play-trains. com/two-color-oil-and-water-discovery-bottles/).
- Tornado bottles – you can purchase Tornado Tubes on Amazon.

Touch

- A child with a hyposensitive tactile system may be overly tactile and need to touch and feel everything in reach, which may be perceived as annoying or intrusive. They relate to their environment through touch. Stimulation-seeking behaviour like deliberately bumping into things is common. The pupil may chew or suck constantly on anything to hand: cuffs, hood strings, pencils, toys and gum. Many use the sensation of certain textures, which others find repellent, to keep calm and this should be modified if socially offensive, such as feeling mucus.
- An extraordinarily high threshold of pain can mean that the pupil may bang their head against the wall, bite themselves, or play roughly with other children or toys – hurting themselves seeking to experience tactile sensory input. They do not react to pain. They are quite capable of carrying on as usual with broken bones or other injuries because they just don't feel them. Being unresponsive to extreme temperatures places them at greater risk because they go outside without coats in the extreme cold and, although their body is visibly shaking with the cold, their brain doesn't register it. In rough play a lack of awareness that they are causing pain to others may be rooted in the belief that the other person experiences the sensation of touch like they do.
- They may also be unaware of losing hold or dropping things.
- This child also has difficulties dressing themselves and manipulating small objects like buttons or zips. Putting on clothes properly, like gloves or tights, may be difficult and they may end up with jumpers on inside out, twisted or back to front.

Strategies

- Draw on sandpaper or cut out letters and numbers in it. The pupil can trace the figures with their forefinger.
- Provide chewy sensory toys or crunchy food like carrots, dry cereals, popcorn, celery, apples, nuts, or crackers. Ask the parent to provide the foods.
- Be aware of touch used as an extra sense to seek information about objects.
- Beware of the tendency to seek sensory input by causing physical harm.
- Support them in PE and at other times when they need to get changed or put their coats on to go outside – either allow them longer time to get dressed or help them.

Taste

- Hypo-gustatory children love strongly flavoured food and may lick objects to seek information about them or present with pica. They may also over-produce saliva and regurgitate food.

Strategies

- Direct them to flavoursome meals at lunchtime.
- Don't react to unusually flavoured food in the snack or lunch box.
- Allow tasty snacks, as required, to calm the pupil.

Smell

- Hypo-olfactory children seek strong smells and will overtly sniff objects or people. They love smelly places like the kitchen or dining hall. In extreme cases their olfactory seeking can be socially unacceptable.
- Those with a hyposensitivity to smell may be unaware of unpleasant odours others react to, or poisons which have a noxious smell.
- They may smell to seek extra information about an object, place or person, which can be a little off-putting if you don't understand why. Remember that their perception of the world is fragmentary.

Strategies

- Tolerance – remember that children who overtly sniff objects or people are seeking sensory information to identify what or who it is.
- If you have a pupil with a favourite smell that helps concentration and keeps them calm, use it, under advice from parents and experts. Aromatherapy strategies can enable the pupil to concentrate by blocking out other stimuli.
- Small pouches containing lavender for calming senses and rosemary for alerting them, for example, are a safe way to introduce the beneficial effects of smell.

Vestibular and Proprioception difficulties are linked, therefore I will list strategies at the end.

Vestibular

- This is concerned with the sense of balance, which helps us coordinate the movement of our eyes, head and bodies. Hypo-vestibular children are in constant motion, can't seem to sit still and are fidgety, rocking the body and shaking their legs. They love speed and spinning and will often 'helicopter' in the playground or run around furiously, swing off branches, roll down slopes, somersault, do cartwheels and play roughly with their peers. They love thrill rides at amusement parks and playground swings, roundabouts and trampolines. They run or hop or dance rather than walk.
- Another side effect of the hypo-vestibular sensory disordered pupil is that they will often tire easily as their bodies are in constant motion. They will often lie down, sit in the W position

and rest their head in their hand or flop on the table. They often have problems with co-ordination and gross motor skills.

Proprioception

- Difficulties in receiving information regarding the movement of muscles means that hyposensitive children are unaware of their bodies in space or time. The movement system – the way the brain perceives the body in space and controls our limbs – may be disordered.
- Poor motor control and gross motor planning means not knowing how to get the brain to tell the body what to do. The pupil may walk with a strange gait or veer off line, unable to change direction without great effort. They may be slow, clumsy, trip up and fall over. Lolling or leaning on a wall or even against another person may be the pupil just trying to rest. Navigating transitions through crowded corridors may be challenging. There is often a lack of co-ordination and the use of inappropriate force, which makes playing team sports in PE difficult, for example kicking a ball too hard or too gently.
- The child has to consciously think about their movements and this makes them slow and clumsy and lacking awareness of how much force is needed to complete an act. Getting dressed is difficult and they may struggle to put their arms into sleeves and draw trousers over their legs without falling over.
- The difficulties with hypo-sensory vestibular and proprioception systems are not confined to gross motor skills and movement but have an impact upon the child's ability to track sentences across a page; letters may be written backwards and they may confuse left and right. Pupils may also have difficulty with deciding what to do and how to do it, never mind 'doing' it.
- Difficulties with movement can also affect fine motor skills: holding a pen, a paintbrush or scissors, and rubbing out mistakes can result in the paper being torn as they apply excessive force to the action. Manipulating cooking utensils, tools and small objects in Technology also causes problems. In areas where there are risks moving around the room and using tools, these pupils need to be supported with a 1-2-1 to keep them safe.
- Writing may be a struggle: the pencil may be pushed too hard and snap. A pupil may have hyper-mobility which is a common trait in AS, and the act of writing my also be painful. Poor motor planning means that writing may need high level conscious thought in order to complete the action. The pupil who is not only having to think consciously how to draw the letter but remember what they are writing about will have real difficulties keeping up with written tasks.
- Strategies that younger children use to regulate their hypo-sensitivities include: stamping, running, dancing, hitting or thumping or shoving something hard; slamming things down; pushing heavy objects like furniture; bumping into walls or people; sitting down heavily; lying under heavy objects like bean bags and squeezing into small spaces. Adapt and incorporate these activities and use them as motivational tools.
- These difficulties can lead to negative feelings: fear of failure and humiliation, frustration, anger and a tendency to give up or refuse to do a task before they have even started. Develop a programme of strategies with the parents and Occupational Therapist. Catering for a pupil's sensory needs may feel like an added burden on an already restricted timetable. However, the rewards will speak for themselves, in helping the pupil to regulate both their behaviour and their ability to concentrate better and learn.

Strategies for Hypo-sensitivity

- Give the pupil space and be flexible, tolerant and patient.
- Timetable sensory activities several times a day.
- Timetable vigorous exercise several times a day: exercises in the classroom – stand and stretch; jumping jacks; marching on the spot; chair push ups; moving heavy furniture; carrying heavy loads.
- In PE pay greater attention to the core skills for these pupils. Be prepared to offer them alternative activities to team sports and complex games. Use this time to feed their senses!
- Activities to build up fine motor skills – pick-up-sticks, chopsticks and dried peas, cross-stitch.
- A laptop or tablet instead of pencil and paper. They will not only find this easier to use but it will also help them to satisfy their need for perfection.
- Timetable noisy activities.
- Stress balls; things to slam, thump, jump on; crushing drinks cans underfoot.
- Move and sit cushions (PhysioRoom New Junior Air Stability Wobble Cushion).
- Thera Band.
- Avoid forcing the pupil to use the same thing as everyone else – meet the needs of the individual pupil.

In each activity in the early years seek opportunities to feed the senses as a normal part of the lesson. Attend to 'hypo' as well as 'hyper' sensitivity. Be alert to the individual's needs at the time – don't fall into the trap of meeting a hypo-sensory need when the pupil needs calming strategies. It is a common myth that individuals suffer from either hyper- or hypo-sensitivity: the reality is that they may suffer from both, depending upon their emotions and environment.

Websites

Sensory diet suggestions: Sensory Diet Prepared by Christy E. Yee, OTR
https://www.autism-mi.org/Portals/0/Documents/Resources/Sensory/Sensory%20Diet.pdf

Summary

The pupil with AS may display a range of negative behaviours because of their sensory issues:

- Distraction and the inability to plan and organize or start or finish a task;
- Poor motor skills and clumsiness;
- Hyperactivity and over-reaction;
- Zoning out and withdrawing;
- Isolation and emotional confusion;
- Agitation and anxiety, frustration and anger;
- Inability to exert self-control;
- Tiring quickly;
- Self-stimulation or self-harm – flapping, hitting the body or head banging.

A lack of awareness of a particular sensitivity and a failure to act can quickly lead to a meltdown. In certain situations, behind the explosive outburst, the anger and frustration is, very likely, a child in pain. They may refuse to do something not because they won't do it but because they *can't* do it.

Use the Sensory Integration Difficulties Checklist (Table 7.1) at the end of this section to ascertain whether your target pupil has any specific difficulties that may impact on their learning or social inclusion. Complete a copy from your observations and send another copy home to be completed by the pupil's parents or carers.

Draw up an Individual Sensory Diet Plan for the pupil (see Table 7.2).

A mainstream school must be absolute hell for children who have sensory integration problems on several levels. Their brains work harder to compensate for the difficulties they experience. Managing the daily assault on their senses means harnessing parts of the brain not usually associated with the function. At the end of the day, having held it all together at school, the child may be utterly exhausted or over-stimulated and go into shutdown or meltdown at home and the parents have to deal with the fallout.

This is one of the reasons why homework is so difficult for the pupil with AS. Apart from the fact that it is quite clearly schoolwork and, therefore, logically, it should be done at school, they may be totally incapable of doing it. While they are in school they rely on a key worker and ever-vigilant staff to help them. They need your *understanding, tolerance* and *patience* and above all to keep them safe.

Self-harm

Self-harm in the younger child may be due to hyposensitivity (rather than low self-esteem) and the need for stimulation, or it may be a personal strategy to block out the pain felt through overload of other senses. 'Telling' a child to stop 'self-harming' rarely works because it serves a beneficial purpose to them. Reducing the levels of anxiety and/or pain will work. Find the reason behind the self-harm and prevent the distress leading to this behaviour, or find ways to distract the child and/or replace the harmful behaviour. Seek expert advice based upon the Autism diagnosis.

Be careful not to add to the distress by preventing behaviour that is distressing for you to watch but which does not actually cause the child any lasting harm, such as hitting the head with the hands. This needs careful consideration, because if you restrain the hands then the child may bang their head against the floor or the wall, which can do a great deal more damage than a hand. Remove the trigger that led to the distress and change the behaviour instead (see Chapter 8).

Table 7.1   Sensory Integration Difficulties Checklist

Pupil:..   Form:...

Age:..   Date:...

1. Auditory System – Sound	Often	Sometimes	Never
Hypersensitivity			
Distracted by imperceptible sounds – lights humming, electrical wires			
Distracted by background noises – chatter, cars, other class's noise			
Starts at unexpected sounds – sirens, shouting			
Frightened of certain sounds – vacuum cleaner, drill, hairdryer			
Puts hands defensively over ears in noisy environments – classroom, halls, cinema, sports events			
Reacts badly to a certain person's voice			
Asks people to be quiet			
Cannot concentrate in a noisy environment			
Becomes agitated and disruptive during noisy activities			
Avoids going to assemblies or participating in large group activities			
Tunes out of what's going on around them			
Relaxes in quiet environment, when spoken to quietly			
Hyposensitivity			
Does not respond to name being called			
Forgets oral instructions immediately			
Does not appear to understand what has been said			
Talks self through a task			
Cannot pinpoint origin of sound			
Cannot hear certain sounds			
Ignores some sounds			
Likes loud music or turns volume up on TV, iPod			
Makes a lot of noise			
Talks loudly			
Hums, coughs, clears throat			

Auditory Processing Difficulties			
Unable to filter out sounds and concentrate on speaker			
Asks speaker to repeat what has just been said			
Cannot fulfil more than one or two instructions at a time			
Does not appear to have understood what has been said			
Difficulty expressing self in words			
Begins a sentence but loses the thread of what is being said			
Interrupts other people in mid flow			
Mispronounces words after hearing them			
Seeks reassurance from listener while talking			

2. Visual System – Sight	Often	Sometimes	Never
Hypersensitivity			
Distressed by bright lights, wears sunglasses indoors			
Difficulty discerning shape/form in busy background			
Distracted by displays, pictures; clouds other visual stimuli			
Distressed by a certain colour or bright tones			
Rubs eyes after reading			
Cannot focus on text, reading and writing tasks			
Avoids eye contact			
Fixated by detail, stares intently at something			
Likes being in a dark room			
Hyposensitivity			
Loses place when reading or doing sequence work e.g. maths problems			
Misreads words, mispronunciation			
Reads words backwards – was = saw,			
Cannot see whole picture, focuses on details/patterns			
Complains about visual disturbance – seeing double, blurred vision			
Poor handwriting – different sized letters, writing along a line			
Poor hand–eye co-ordination when cutting out or drawing shapes			

3. Tactile System – Touch	Often	Sometimes	Never
Hypersensitive			
Reacts to a light touch as if it hurt, rubs the place touched			
Dislikes being touched, won't touch another person			
Stands apart from others, withdraws from when approached			
Rolls up sleeves, frequently adjusts clothes			
Intolerant of certain textures, wool, labels in clothing, socks, hats			
Dislikes having hair cut or brushed, nails clipped, teeth brushed			
Cannot tolerate messy play – paint, sand, dough, glue			
Walks on tiptoes			
Dislikes new shoes or walking barefoot on grass, sand			
Distressed by water on face when swimming or washing face			
Dislikes certain textures of food and refuses to eat them			
Oversensitive to heat or cold			
Hyposensitive			
Touches everything and everyone, rubs hands together			
Hands in pockets			
Sits on hands			
Unaware of minor cuts and abrasions, high tolerance of pain			
Doesn't feel the cold, refuses to wear a coat out			
Seeks rough textures and revels in messy play			
Rough when playing with other children or pets			
Unaware of bumping into others – just barges past people			
Unaware of being dirty or snotty			
Seeks textural stimulation – repeated stroking of clothing or blanket, rubs body along walls			
May hit or pinch themselves repeatedly, scratches, rubs, hits, pulls hair, bangs head against wall			

4. Vestibular System – Balance	Often	Sometimes	Never
Hypersensitive			
Poor balance when moving, sits down often			
Dislikes playground activities on equipment			
Afraid of heights, even small ones – kerb			
Clumsy – falls over often			
Seems cautious when moving around, holds onto wall, railings, other people			
Avoids making rapid changes of direction			
May complain of feeling sick during physical activities			
Has difficulty riding a bike			
Hyposensitive			
Hyperactive, paces up and down			
Loves spinning, swinging, bouncing			
Impulsive and seeks thrills			
Always runs, jumps and rushes ahead of everyone			
Moves when sitting – rocking, leg shaking, head wags			
Turns upside down on chair			
Craves rapid movement			
Enjoys rough rides – amusement parks, on bike			

5. Proprioceptive System – Movement	Often	Sometimes	Never
Lacks Awareness of Movement and Appropriate Force			
Written work is untidy			
May break pencil by pressing too hard			
Frequently tears the paper when rubbing out			
Often breaks things			
Hurts people unintentionally with force of grip			
Uses too much force for everyday activities – stamping, slamming, yanking, shoving			
Seeks Sensory Input			
Tight clothing			
Stamps feet			
Chews fingers, pencils, clothing			
Crashes into things deliberately			
Cracks knuckles frequently			
Rough play with other children – hitting, bumping, shoving			
Leans heavily on things or people			

Poor Co-ordination and Poor Muscle Tone			
Weak grip			
Poor motor skills, fine and gross			
Tires easily			
Difficulty doing up buttons or zip			

6. Gustatory System – Taste	Often	Sometimes	Never
Hypersensitive			
Picky eater – sticks to same food day after day in lunchbox, same dish in restaurants			
Can discern change in ingredients or wrong flavours – fishy flavour in bacon or chicken			
Prefers bland foods			
Only able to eat so much food, e.g. chocolate – too tasty			
Dislikes toothpaste			
Eats only hot or cold food			
Hyposensitive			
Chews clothing, pencils and other inedible objects			
Likes heavily flavoured food – salt, pepper, chilli			
Puts non-edible objects into mouth, chews string, paper, clothing			

7. Olfactory System – Smell	Often	Sometimes	Never
Hypersensitive			
Smells odours which go unnoticed by others			
Offended/nauseated by bodily odours			
Perfume/deodorants may be irritating			
Refusal to go into science labs, tech rooms or houses because of smell			
Likes or dislikes someone because of the way they smell			
Hyposensitive			
Doesn't appear to notice foul odours			
Overtly sniffs things to smell them			

Further Comments ....

....

....

....

....

....

....

....

....

....

Signed .... Date ....

Relationship to pupil ....

Sensory Integration Difficulties Summary and Actions

Pupil:.. Form:..

Age:.. Date:..

Hyper-Sensitivities	Effect Upon Pupil	Action Taken

Hypo-Sensitivities	Effect Upon Pupil	Action Taken

Table 7.2   Sensory Diet Plan – Hypersensory regulation

Name:............................   Class:...............   Teacher:........................   Key Support Worker:..................

Note activity in Activity row and mark off the number of times activity done in rows opposite the day.

Activity							
Monday							
Tuesday							
Wednesday							
Thursday							
Friday							
Activity							
Monday							
Tuesday							
Wednesday							
Thursday							
Friday							
Activity							
Monday							
Tuesday							
Wednesday							
Thursday							
Friday							
Activity							
Monday							
Tuesday							
Wednesday							
Thursday							
Friday							

Sensory audit

After completing the Sensory Checklist, conduct a Environmental Audit (see Table 7.3) of the spaces the pupil will be using in relation to their hypersensitivities. Reducing the sensory assault will help them concentrate.

Consider:

- The physical space of the areas in the school the child will be going into; how will it impact upon them – noise, light, colour, smell and movement?
- Does each space have a safe, sensorially dampened area where you can place the child, before they become overwhelmed?
- Transition around the school – will the child be able to get from one place to the other without distress?
- School staff – are they quietly spoken? Shouters can cause the child to freeze and be unable to respond. Shouting at a child with autism can cause an insult to their sensory system and generate a high level of fear and anxiety whenever that person is in the same room as they are. Are the people who work with the child calm, quiet and prepared to meet the child's needs?

Table 7.3 Environmental Audit

Name:		Classroom:		Teacher:		Possible Solutions
Sights	Lights	Displays/Colour	Clutter	Windows	Reflections	Position in class Carel/workstation
Sounds	Bells/Fire Alarm	Electrical Equipment	Nearby Classrooms	Hall, Gym, Dining Hall	Open windows	Warnings Switch off electrics Dampeners Ear plugs Sound proofing
Smells	Glue, Paint, Cleaning Materials	Perfume, Deodorant Bodies	Food	Open Windows	Toilets	Staff avoid strong perfume Alternative toilet

Category						Possible Solutions
Taste	Food	Pica	Identifying Objects			Special diet
Touch	Clothing	People light touch	Glue, Paints	Food	Seating	Loose clothing Labels removed
Space and Movement	Hypermobility	Transition	Queuing	Dining Area	Changing Room	Weighted Cushion Exercise
Other	Voices	Personal Space				Change TA or teacher

Further reading

Myles, B.S., Cook, K.T., Miller, N.E., Rinner, L. and Robbins, L.A. (2005 reprint). *Asperger Syndrome and Sensory Issues: practical solutions for making sense of the world.* Kansas: Autism Asperger Publishing Co.

Websites

A is for Autism, BBC Four: http://www.youtube.com/watch?v=cPR2H4Zd8bl
   http://www.sensory-processing-disorder.com/
Sensory Overload Simulation – WeirdGirlCyndi http://www.youtube.com/watch?v=BPDTEuotHe0
A Child's View of Sensory Processing – ESGWNRM http://www.youtube.com/watch?v=D1G5ssZlVUw
http://musingsofanaspie.com/2013/06/18/a-cognitive-defense-of-stimming-or-why-quiet-hands-
   makes-math-harder/

Sensory breaks: The sensory room

It is worth repeating that while some pupils with AS appear to manage the typical school day, a short conversation with parents may tell a different story. Many families report that they meltdown, in response to the stress of the school day, when they get home. It's like living through a tornado, as the child either seeks the sensory stimulation they have been denied in school or 'hides' until they have restored themselves. Some sleep for a whole day to recover from the assault on their fragile nervous system.

If you can manage the sensory environment you will reduce stress and anxiety and help them manage their emotions and behaviour. So if your school doesn't have a sensory room already, it would make a great project for the Technology department.

Useful tools to have in a sensory room are:

- lava or bubble lamps, coloured lights and glitter ball;
- conventional or daylight bulbs to replace any strip or neon lighting;
- mp3 player to play favourite music or sounds, for example running water or a storm, from the pupil's iPod or SEN resources;
- if loud music is needed, let them listen to it on their iPod;
- aromatherapy oils;
- a texture wall or tapestry with different textured materials and cushions made from different materials such as velvet and space blanket material;
- a swing hammock;
- large cushions or beanbags to lie on or snuggle under;
- weighted blankets;
- stress balls to knead;
- padded mats for a space on the floor to roll around on;
- and a pop-up tent.

These are suggested to stimulate or calm all the senses. Does your pupil have a sensory room at home? What works best for the pupil? Ask them what they would like to see, touch, listen to, smell and do in there.

Another effective, calming tool is a fish tank with brightly coloured fish. This may also be used to support an interest.

Time out in the sensory room should be timetabled, not a reactive therapy, so that the pupil can reset their nervous system regularly. Activities should be designed to meet the individual pupil's needs and drawn up in consultation with an OT.

Never ever use the room for punishment or lock the child in it: it is a refuge, a place to calm down, not an isolation unit. To place a child in a room and lock the door is unlawful imprisonment. *The child should never be forced to go into a sensory room*. They should always be able to leave when they wish, as they may be aware of over-stimulation that you cannot see. Alternative areas and activities should be available to meet the pupil's needs, such as a walk outdoors, or exercises in the hall or gym.

A member of staff should also be in the room guiding activities. In order to safeguard the child and to keep pupils and staff safe, monitor what goes on in the room by installing a discreet video monitoring system.

You can find good ideas on the Internet for sensory rooms, equipment, and companies that design and create sensory rooms for schools.

Top Tip

Play music unobtrusively in the classroom to enhance levels of concentration and reduce unnecessary chatter. The music should be a single instrument and played at low volume.

Sensory snacks

Timetabling sensory snacks into the day will reduce stress levels. These should be tailored to the individual pupil's needs based on the feedback from the sensory checklist, with input from an OT. Meeting an AS pupil's needs to regulate their fragile nervous system is not a reward or an excuse to get out of doing work. Feeding this need will enable them to focus and achieve.

Sensory Snacks	
Calming Senses	**Alerting Senses**
Sounds: classical music, whale song, rhythm, heartbeat, water trickling over rocks, thunderstorm	Rousing music – heavy metal, playing a musical instrument, dance music, marching tunes – Grand Old Duke of York
Silence, reading, drawing	Dancing, running from one end of the gym to the other, stamping, thumping, pounding, drumming
Slow moving lights, fire light, lava lamps, fish tank	Flashing lights
Rocking chair, hammock	Swinging – quickly, changing direction
Wear rucksack with heavy books	Wear rucksack with heavy books
Jobs about the school: clean boards, errands, washing up, sorting cupboards	Jumping – trampoline
Textures – bowl of rice, sand, water, different materials	Weights room, lie under heavy cushions or weighted blankets
Squeeze ball, fidget	Moving heavy furniture, pushing against the wall
Sit or lie in a dark tent	Rolling on the floor
Wrapped tightly	Climbing bars
Chewing or sucking toy	Eating carrots, crisps
Pet club	Gardening club

The sensory box

Make a personalized sensory box to use discreetly in lessons. Place a number of articles in a shoe or tissue box with a discreet entry through the top or side. It should contain things the pupil likes the feel/smell/taste/look of. You don't have to spend money on sensory toys: include day-to-day objects that will help keep the pupil's senses ordered, for example textured cloth, strings of beads, sponges, small cuddly toys, wood blocks, Blu Tac, stress ball. Ask the parents what sensory toys they have in the car or at home. Ask the pupil what they would like to 'fiddle' with.

8 The real challenge – managing behaviour

There are two attitudes to challenging behaviour: either
the child **is** a problem,
or
the child **has** a problem.

Dixie Jordan (2008)

Behaviour is actions that can be observed, measured and repeated.

Is the term 'challenging' used to describe the child challenging authority or to describe the challenge for the child in managing their behaviour?

Using the term 'challenging' to describe the behaviour of a child with a neuro-physiological condition does not acknowledge the real difficulties the child has in processing what is happening and being able to respond to it rationally. Social and language confusion, sensory overload, extreme anxieties arising from the need to meet demands within the time given in a pressurised environment such as a school, are the conditions under which pupils on the spectrum are trying to function and, sometimes, they just can't cope and panic.

ASCs are hidden disabilities and this makes it difficult for NT people to imagine what difficulties the person is experiencing. There are many myths surrounding autistic behaviour: they are just naughty children; they will grow out of it; they have tantrums; they have annoying habits; they are rude; they can control their behaviour; it's caused by poor discipline at home.

Parents develop strategies to manage behaviour at home, pre and post diagnosis, to keep them safe and able to function to the best of their ability. Post diagnosis, a parent will often learn as much as they can about the condition and the strategies they can use to help their child and they are very successful. Autistic children process the world differently and schools should make adjustments to enable the child to do as best they can, despite these strategies appearing to be 'giving in' to the 'unreasonable' demands the child makes.

The nature of autism, in particular the fragile neurological system whereby the brain takes in too much information and cannot process it fast enough; nor is it able to filter out the resulting overload of sensory input; this causes extreme distress to the young child, who has not learned how to regulate their physical or emotional response or be able to inhibit it. This may be a reaction to a situation or event, especially if it was unexpected, and may result in panic and physical outburst, or even catatonia, where they freeze and are unable to do anything, as in an epileptic, petit mal seizure.

Elvén (2010) defines challenging behaviour as:

'behaviour that causes problems for people around the person'.

Most behaviour is a form of communication, or it serves a function by leading to an outcome.

'What is this person trying to communicate to me?'

and

'What are they hoping to achieve by doing this?' are the questions we need to ask ourselves.

Challenging behaviour is motivated by two factors:

- The need to feel *safe*. Feeling threatened or intimidated by something in the environment may automatically trigger a reaction.
- To gain something. The pupil may have learned that they can get what they want if they behave in a certain way. For example, an older brother is playing with a toy they want to play with, so they cry. To stop the crying the child is given the toy they wanted.

Habit may also play a part in triggering the challenging behaviour in response to a certain situation, because of its association with a place, routine, other people...

When working with a child who experiences the world in a different way and is struggling to make sense of it, or protect themselves, we need to consider carefully what we can do to help them feel safe and able to learn. The way in which they communicate with us may confuse us by their focus on the outcome and lead us to believe that we are being manipulated. Often they are so distressed that they cannot give us a reason and we make our own judgements, which are very often negative.

Look at it from the child's perspective:

S/he's 'lazy' = I don't understand what they want me to do; what if I fail?

and

S/he's disobedient = I can't do this. I'm scared. I don't know what's going to happen next.

It is very important to remember that the child is doing the best they can in the circumstances. It is our job to find out what is making it difficult for them to manage and to change things to support them. This may be dealing with the fear of walking down the corridor to the dining hall at lunchtime. The child with autism would rather not eat than have to walk through crowds of people into a noisy dining area where they have to queue with lots of other people pushing around them.

People who work with young children with AS need to have a high level of tolerance and understand that the behaviour is part of the way in which they communicate. In some situations it may be the only way they can communicate their emotions.

Never underestimate the effort it will take the child to try and adapt to the new environment, and the emotional and physical toll upon them. The support you need to give the child may seem extreme and unnecessary, but if it isn't there it can take only a few weeks before the child, exhausted by trying to meet your expectations, simply cannot cope and may start to meltdown or be unable to do as they are told. If you consider this an outright refusal, disobedience or bad behaviour – think again. Ask yourself, is it: 'I *won't* do it' or 'I *can't* do it'?

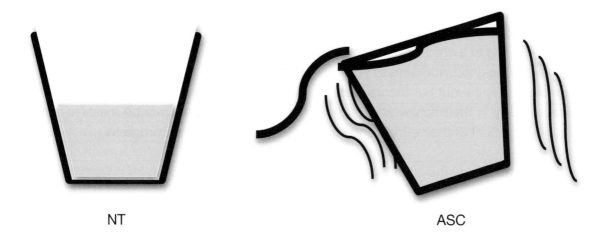

NT   ASC

Tony Attwood describes the stress bucket as being half full for a NT: always full for the person with AS which may, without warning, overflow!

Heading off a meltdown by distracting the pupil with a favourite activity or what may be perceived as a 'reward' goes against everything we are taught. If a pupil cannot regulate their behaviour, we see it as our duty to impose our own discipline. We may have problems with the choice of strategy a pupil uses in an attempt to calm themself. It may be seen as oppositional or avoidance behaviour: a refusal to do as they are asked; or rewarding what we see as 'bad' behaviour.

When we are trying to prevent a meltdown we should use whatever means we can to effect a good outcome, not only for the pupil but for the whole class and yourself. In this instance, a good outcome is to avoid a meltdown using whatever does the job of helping the child calm down and regain self-control.

It is not a power struggle. We often make the mistake of thinking we have to control others to get them to do what we want. Rather, it is about enabling the pupil to make the right decision: to want to do what you want, to co-operate and work towards the same goal. It is the pupil's sense of wellbeing that matters, their self-confidence and belief that they can do what is demanded of them. If they believe they can, they will attempt it and, in all likelihood, succeed.

If it is too difficult, they fear the consequences of failure, become distressed, frustrated and angry; and their behaviour may become oppositional and defiant. This is the tipping point – the next action you make can result in calming the situation or escalating the problem, which will lead to confrontation and meltdown.

Are you the right person for the job?

This is not meant to be a provocative question. If you haven't worked with autistic children before, you are entering into a completely different world. In order to do the best by your pupil with AS you will have to go more than half way to establish a relationship of mutual respect and trust.

The qualities you will need are:

Knowledge about autism;
Understanding about autism and how it impacts on your target child;
Tolerance of the behaviour that is part of autism;
Patience – be prepared to repeat instructions and teach skills over and over and over again… and then again and again.

Calm demeanour;
Modification of your own **behaviour** and **language;**
Honesty – lying to a child with autism is tantamount to a betrayal; never tell an autistic pupil they have done good work unless you can justify your praise.
Empathy – they cannot put themselves into your shoes: can you wear theirs?
Pride and **Joy** in their achievements, however small; for them it will be massive and your acknowledgement of their efforts and successes is the key to their progress.

Are you ready to include the child with autism into your school? Do you:

- Accept that their difficulties are part of the condition?
- Respect that they will do their best?
- Are you prepared to protect them from sensory overload and social confusion by making adjustments and giving them the tools necessary to making them feel safe, accepted and able to do what is asked of them?

If so, you are more than half way there to having a successful transition and establishing good autism practice that will enable the child to make good progress under your care.

Planning

Plan carefully before the child arrives in school. If you have had experience of working with children on the spectrum, you will already appreciate that autism impacts upon each child in a different way; no two children present with the same behaviours. It will take a considerable amount of time to prepare for each pupil at the outset, but the positives far outweigh the negatives. Focusing upon the needs of the individual child will enhance your understanding of their difficulties and how to overcome them.

Research

With all the information you have gathered about the child during transition, you can prepare to support them when they attend the school.

Communication with parents is vital when managing the behaviour of a child with autism. They will already have strategies in place at home, and if these can be consistently applied at school there is a better chance of achieving a successful outcome.

It will also set up a working partnership for the development of further strategies devised to support at home the work done in school. Never underestimate the value of maintaining a good working relationship with the parents.

Before term starts have clear strategies in place and everyone prepared to apply them across the school. Areas for consideration are:

- Physical Environmental Assessment
- Sensory Support Plan
- Behavioural Support Plan (BSP)
- Differentiation of lessons
- Language modification.

Strategies

Physical environment

Having collected all the information available about the pupil, adapt the environment to minimize the effect it has upon them and enable the pupil to learn and socialize.

Sensory Support Plan

Using the information recorded from a sensory checklist, timetable sensory snacks to meet their needs. Many schools offer a safe haven for break times but it may be better use of that time to attend to sensory needs and let them exercise, especially if they have been sitting for long periods of time.

Behaviour Support Plan

If the child has difficulties managing aspects of their behaviour before they arrive in the school, it is sensible to have a BSP in place before they arrive. Also, give some thought to how you can modify your own behaviour.

Think ahead to situations that will present difficulties for the pupil on the autism spectrum, due to a lack of organization skills, but that can be prepared for in advance:

- where to hang up a coat;
- going to the toilet – the child may not recognize the physical signs and will have to be prompted to go at regular intervals during the day;
- forgotten something – homework, pencil case, PE kit;
- fire alarm goes off;
- substitute teacher;
- change of room;
- change to timetable or routine;
- bullying: how to recognize it and what to do about it.

Use Template 8.1 to help the pupil work out what they do 'If'… in the everyday situations that cause problems for the pupil in school. A child with autism rarely learns by observation or intuition. They need to be taught exactly what to do in every single situation and repeatedly over time. They cannot transfer skills from one scenario to another. If it is sunny one day and they have learned to do something that they are then asked to repeat another day when it is raining, it will be a completely new experience and they will have to learn it all over again. In order to help reinforce the lesson, it is important to give the instruction in exactly the same way as before.

Describe a possible scenario (Template 8.1):

If I want to go to the toilet.
I put up my hand and ask the teacher
or I show the teacher my card.

A more complex scenario for a younger child may be:

If I forget my PE kit.

This strategy needs to be developed in consultation with parents to ensure that they can fulfill it, if it involves getting the kit to school. Remember, if the parents are also on the spectrum, they too may have problems with organization.

No PE kit = No PE.
Get PE kit. How?
a) Go to reception (picture)
b) Telephone my mum/dad
c) Mum/dad bring PE kit to school.

Put it on a key fob so that they can refer to it. This will help if it is a recurring difficulty. (See the template below.)

If you have never done a BSP before, this website has an excellent outline of how to prepare one for a pupil on the autism spectrum:

http://www.education.vic.gov.au/Documents/about/programs/bullystoppers/bspguidelines.pdf

Going to the toilet.

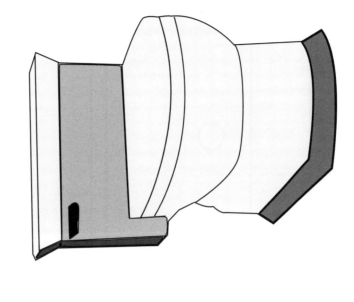

I go back to class.

I wash my hands.

I have a funny feeling between my legs.

I feel wriggly.

I cross my legs.

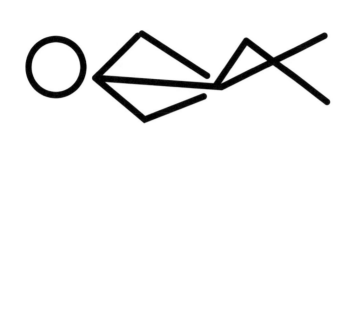

This means that...

I go to the toilet.

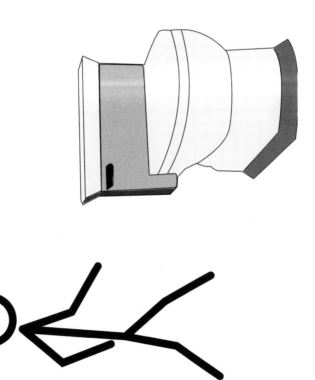

I want to go to the toilet.

I put up my hand

Toilet, please.

I say

Template 8.2

If

Photo of
Key TA

Differentiation of lessons

Be prepared for some children with ASC to be considerably more advanced than the average pupil in some subjects and weaker in others. The ASC profile can be very spiky. Work to their strengths.

The pupil may have real difficulties doing the work set. For example: writing a story about a pet – the anxieties surrounding this are many: How do I start? What do I write about? How do I finish?; Teacher hates my handwriting; My hand hurts when I write; I don't have a pet...

- Break down tasks.
- Use visual supports – avoid long, spoken instructions.
- Use the pupil's interests to help focus on the task.
- Don't bore your pupil – in some subjects they may struggle, in others excel.

Language modification

This is very much something you can do to facilitate communication and understanding and it will be discussed in detail in Chapter 11. However, in brief:

- Keep it simple.
- Say exactly what you mean.
- Avoid changing words if you repeat the instruction.
- Allow time for processing.

Further reading

Elvén, B. H. (2010). *No Fighting, No Biting, No Screaming: How to make behaving positively possible for people with autism and other developmental disabilities*. London, Jessica Kingsley Publishers.

When the behaviour becomes a challenge

Functions of behaviour

There is always a reason behind the functional behaviour of a child:

- **Medical** – rule this out first. Use the body template to help you assess where and what the problem is. Use several descriptions of stomach pain related to specific conditions. It's like a ball:
  - rolling around: feeling sick in the stomach;
  - bouncing: anxiety;
  - with knobs: stomach ache;
  - with a spike: acute pain;
  - floating around: feeling nervous;
  - a bubbly tummy: diarrhoea.
- **Inattention** – I can look at you or I can listen but I can't do both things at once.

- **Social attention** – seeking a reaction from those around them.
- **Achieve a specific goal** – to do a certain activity or get away from the environment.
- **Avoidance** – to stop doing an activity or work; get out of the environment.
- **Sensory stimulation** – to feed a sensory need.
- **Boredom** – they have learned the lesson, get all their answers right and do not see the point of doing it over again.
- **Need to control** what is happening around them because they cannot predict or infer from your instructions or actions what is going to happen next. They are frightened.

Where does it hurt?

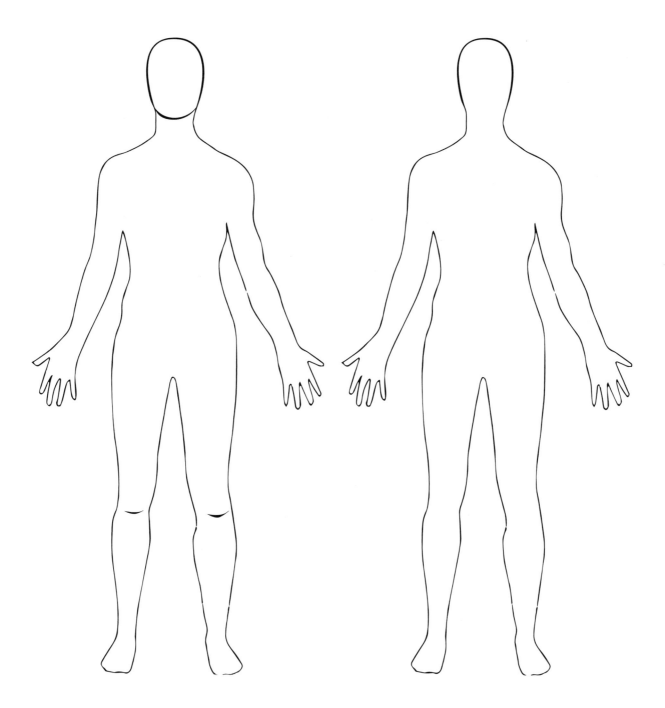

Functional Behavioural Analysis

1 Identify the behaviour.
2 Analyse the behaviour.
3 Respond to the behaviour.
4 Positive behaviour intervention.

The pupil with an ASC is likely to arrive in school with a number of behaviours that you find unacceptable and it is foolish to try and change everything at once. Using Rita Adair's (Norfolk County Council) Disruptive Behaviour Checklist will help to identify the behaviour that requires attention. As is suggested at the end of the checklist, focus on one or two behaviours at a time and no more.

Follow this up with a STAR Analysis to effect the best outcome. If you have to put a behaviour intervention in place, you need to understand what motivates the behaviour.

Use the Behaviour Assessment Chart to record incidents over a period of time. It can take time to discern patterns and this will help to complete an effective analysis.

Norfolk County Council

CHECKLIST OF DISRUPTIVE BEHAVIOUR

This information is to help us identify the specific disruptive behaviours displayed by the pupil. Please tick each of the following behaviours in the appropriate column.

A = Average occurrence for pupils in class
+ = More frequent than for average pupil
− = Less frequent than for average pupil

Please mark with an asterisk any behaviour that you consider to occur in extreme form or with excessive frequency.

Name:	Form:	Date:	−	A	+
A 1 Turns round in seat					
2 Rocks in chair					
3 Sits out of position in seat					
4 Fidgets					
5 Plays with toys or possessions					
6 Shuffles chair					
7 Stands up					
8 Changes seat					
9 Moves from seat					
10 Walks about class					
11 Runs about class					
12 Leaves classroom					
13 Climbs on furniture					
14 Lies on floor					
15 Crawls on floor					

			−	A	+
B 1 Moves furniture					
2 Throws pellets/papers					
3 Throws equipment/books					
4 Throws furniture					
5 Bangs furniture					
6 Stamps feet					
7 Taps hand on furniture					
8 Taps pencil/ruler					

			−	A	+
C 1 Cries					
2 Laughs/giggles inappropriately					
3 Makes non-verbal noises					
4 Whistles					
5 Sings					
6 Tells lies					
7 Pulls funny faces					
8 Makes inappropriate gestures					
9 Talks to self					

Name:	Form:	Date:	−	A	+
D 1 Damages own work					
2 Damages own property					
3 Damages class furniture/equipment					
4 Writes on furniture					
5 Writes on wall					
6 Spits on floor					
7 Deliberately disarranges dress					
8 Hurts self					
9 Feigns illness					
10 Feigns need to go to toilet					
11 Plays with or strikes matches					
12 Damages others' property					
13 Takes others' property					
14 Interferes with teachers' property					

E 1 Carries on distracting conversation with other pupil					
2 Shouts at other pupil					
3 Verbally abuses other pupils					
4 Spits at other pupil					
5 Obliquely assaults another, e.g. drawing pin on chair					
6 Mimics other pupil					
7 Strikes with hand another pupil					
8 Strikes with weapon another pupil					
9 Pokes another pupil					
10 Kicks another pupil					
11 Pushes another pupil					
12 Trips another pupil					
13 Bites another pupil					
14 Scratches another pupil					
15 Pinches another pupil					
16 'Strangles' another pupil					
17 Clings to another pupil					
18 Verbally threatens other pupil					
19 Physically threatens other pupil					

Name:			Form:	Date:	–	A	+
F 1	Carries on distracting conversation with teacher						
2	Calls out to teacher						
3	Shouts at teacher						
4	Mimics teacher						
5	Verbally abuses teacher under breath						
6	Verbally abuses teacher directly						
7	Clings to teacher						
8	Assaults teacher obliquely, e.g. practical joke						
9	Assaults teacher directly						
10	Verbally threatens teacher						
11	Physically threatens teacher						
12	Fails to follow teachers' instructions						
13	Refuses to attempt work						
14	Arrives late						
15	Leaves coat on						
16	Packs away early						
17	Fails to leave classroom						

G – Any Other (Please specify)			

The checklist can be used as a stand-alone resource by schools working with parents/carers, or in conjunction with advice/consultation from external professionals. It is designed to assist in identifying priority behaviour targets to address and is particularly suitable for use in early intervention. It can also be used to plan progression to other aspects of behaviour causing concern as progress is made with initial targets.

Strategies to address the target behaviours should be developed in the context of possible causes, which may be external to the pupil or the school.

Name:	Form:	Date:

Priority behaviours to target

1

2

Teacher's name: .... Date: ....

Suggestions for reasons behind the behaviour may be found here related to different Tiers: http://www.schools.norfolk.gov.uk/Behaviour-and-safety/Behaviour/index.htm.

Reproduced with permission from Rita Adair, Senior Lead Educational Psychologist, Educational Psychology and Specialist Support, Norfolk Children's Services.

Functional Behaviour Analysis using the STAR method

Having completed the checklist, conduct FBA analysis using the STAR (Setting Conditions, Triggers, Actions and Results) method, developed by Clements and Zarkowska (1994).

The STAR analysis takes a scientific approach. It is important to conduct it rigorously. It should also be noted that identifying triggers and patterns in behaviour may take some time in order to gain a clear understanding of what is really happening and why. Then replace the challenging behaviour with a Functionally Equivalent Replacement Behaviour (FERB). FERBs are desirable/acceptable behaviours that achieve the same result as a less desirable, problem behaviour.

There are four things to take into consideration: Setting Conditions or influences that explain the behaviour, Triggers, Actions and Results. These must be measured in a quantifiable way, describing the behaviour/s in detail and recording:

- Frequency – How often it takes place.
- Rate – How often during a specific time frame – in a minute or 10 minutes.
- Duration – Note how long the behaviour(s) lasts, from start to finish.
- Latency – The time between the Trigger and the onset of the behaviour.
- Magnitude – How intense was the behaviour?

Setting conditions

These are internal and external to the pupil being assessed, reflecting the pupil's ability to meet demands made upon them at the time of the incident.

1   External influences may include:
   - Physical Environment – noise, lighting, temperature; uncomfortable clothing or shoes.
   - Activity – does the individual want to participate or not; stimulation – type and the level.
   - Life Events – bereavement; life changes – e.g. moving home, new school; trauma – e.g. accident, bullying…
   - Social Climate: breakdown in relationships – family, friends; conflict and hostility – personality clashes, bullying, argument with another person; lack of control; or unnecessarily strict control.
2   Internal, personal and emotional influences may include:
   - Poor organization skills
   - Lack of social understanding
   - Confusion – unable to organize and process thoughts
   - Disordered Sensory Processing
   - Inability to self-regulate
   - Poor working memory
   - Impulsivity
   - Poor health
   - Pain
   - Low self-esteem
   - Anxiety, fear, sadness and depression
   - Boredom…

These may be part of the impact having autism and any other co-condition has upon the individual pupil.

Triggers

These are 'things' that set off a particular set of reactions that occur just before the behaviour takes place. These may be particularly difficult to isolate and may include:

- Change of routine
- A particular person
- Pressure to complete the task
- Not wanting to do the task or activity
- Desire
- Need
- Threat.

Actions

These are the challenging behaviours that can be seen by another person. These may be separate behaviours or a behaviour cluster. Whichever, they should be noted in the order in which they occur to identify whether the behaviour is sequential and escalating.

Results

These are the consequences of the behaviour for the individual – did they meet the pupil's needs or desires? The results or outcomes may be positive, negative or neutral. Results should not be confused with action taken by another person, like discipline or punishment.

Use the Behaviour Observation Chart to record your observations in preparation for conducting a STAR Analysis. Detail the pupil's actions. Avoid terms like 'rude'.

Before starting the analysis, collect historical information surrounding their physical or emotional states and the developmental level of the pupil's current skills: ability to learn; work independently; social interaction and personal independence or whether the pupil needs to be supported with cues or prompts. Do they have skills that can be transferred to support alternatives to the challenging behaviour? Identify powerful motivators.

Once you have the information, use different coloured pens to analyze whether the challenging behaviour fulfills a *desire* or a *need* for safety, or both. If it is a need for safety the primary consideration and response should be to ensure that the pupil feels safe. If it is to fulfill a desire then the response should be to fulfill the desire in a more appropriate way with FERB. Another thing to consider is whether the behaviour has become a habit, in which case replacing it with a FERB will be trickier.

Strength list

Zarkowska and Clements recommend writing a list of strengths, which should include:

- Pupil's skills and levels of attainment.
- Pupil's preferences – i.e. powerful motivators.
- Conditions which inspire positive behaviour in the pupil.
- Conditions under which the pupil learns best.

Formulation

What are the factors connected to the developing of the challenging behaviour?
What are the factors involved in maintaining the challenging behaviour?
Include the following details:

- The challenging behaviours.
- Results the challenging behaviours appear to achieve.
- Triggers that initiate them.
- Environmental setting conditions.
- Personal setting conditions.
- Related lack of skills: difficulties with communication, learning and social interaction skills.

Complete the Formulation table

Finally, complete a Statement of Needs to prioritize teaching objectives and devise a behavioural support plan. Do not look at the pupil's deficits but consider the skills they already have and how these can be developed. Look at long-term goals and short-term targets and be SMART! Targets should be: Specific, Measurable, Achievable, Realistic and Time-related.

Replacing challenging behaviour with appropriate behaviour can take a long time, especially if it is a habit and the behaviour works in other settings. Talk to the parents and develop a strategy, which can be used at home and at school. The behaviour may be employed in different setting conditions. Consider the external and internal environment. A pupil's challenging behaviour may be as a result of the way they feel, not just where they are.

Social stories or a symbol card on the table in front of the pupil could prompt the desired behaviour.

Example:
Problem behaviour: pupil shouts to gain your attention. If you respond by giving the pupil the attention s/he wants, the pupil will always shout to gain attention.

Desired behaviour: you want the pupil to put their hand up to gain attention *and* wait quietly. The pupil wants attention immediately.

In order to change the pupil's behaviour, the pupil's desire needs to be met with the FERB. So when the pupil puts their hand up, they must gain your attention immediately because this is functionally equivalent to shouting out – it serves to fulfill the desire.

However, this is not the whole solution because both people's goals must be met. Your goal is for the pupil to learn to put their hand up *and* to wait for your attention.

Don't ignore the problem behaviour, shouting out, but only respond when they use the FERB that you need to teach them: putting up a hand.

The next step would be to teach the new skill of waiting. You acknowledge the raising of the hand immediately but tell the pupil to wait by saying, 'Mike, I am helping Tom. When I have finished, I will help you.' You must fulfill your promise and help Mike as soon as you have finished with Tom and not make Mike wait too long to get attention.

Once that has been reinforced, the pupil may find that putting up the hand does not get acknowledged verbally but you give a signal to the pupil that they will get the attention by a certain time, indicating when the pupil will receive the attention. Again, this desire must be fulfilled, although the time may increase in order to teach waiting.

The next stage is that the need for attention is not acknowledged but you attend to the pupil when you are ready and the pupil knows that you will attend to them when it is their turn.

In this scenario a setting condition is: the pupil with AS has a poor working memory and will need attention immediately or, by the time you get round to them, they will have forgotten what they put their hand up for, followed by the inevitable fallout. You may need to modify your behaviour to meet the needs of the pupil.

If the FERB doesn't work and the behaviour continues, you have probably failed to identify the trigger. Go back and look at the analysis again. What other common factors appear to have been overlooked? Tom sitting next to the same pupil each time he calls out; Mr Perkins is always the same teacher; it is always a hot day; it is always before break or lunch… These types of common factors may suggest that the motivation to call out for attention may be more complex than a simple desire for attention. Complete a Pupil Self Assessment Form (see below).

Does Tom feel safe sitting next to that pupil? Does Mr Perkins always respond to Tom? Is Tom too hot and cannot concentrate? Is the sun shining in his face? Is Tom trying to ask for help because he hates going out to break but can't ask for it? Detailed FBA will highlight these other issues and support finding the problem and solving it.

When selecting an appropriate FERB, we must first understand the function of the problem behaviour. Once the function of the problem behaviour is clearly identified, an appropriate alternative response, or repertoire of alternative responses, can be selected that are equal in function to the targeted challenging behaviour. Alternative responses should be selected based on their social validity and must achieve the same aim in the same time or with less effort. If you replace the behaviour with something more difficult and/or less effective, it won't be used.

Create opportunities to practise new skills using the FERB. Begin with situations that cannot fail because you are there to support and correct the problem. Sabotage situations to challenge them to use the FERB by blocking completion of a task or interrupting a sequence. Don't forget to reinforce the appropriate behaviour by acknowledging their success in using it.

This section has been written in detail with the kind permission of John Clements.

Further reading

Clements, J. and Zarkowska, E. (1994). *Problem Behaviour and People with Severe Learning Disabilities: The S.T.A.R. Approach.* London: Chapman and Hall.

Clements, J. and Zarkowska, E. (2000). *Behavioural Concerns and Autistic Spectrum Disorders: Explanations and strategies for change.* London: Jessica Kingsley Publishers.

Template 8.3 – STAR Functional Behaviour Analysis

Behaviour Observation Chart

Name: .... Form: .... Date: .... Staff initials: ....

Date	Time	Setting Conditions	Trigger	Action	Result

STAR Analysis of Problematic Behaviour: The Formulation

Name:		Form:	Date:	Initials:

Definition of problem behaviour:

Appears to achieve the following results:

Appears to be set off by the following triggers:

Seems to occur in the context of the following environmental setting conditions

Physical: Occupational:

Appears to be related to the following personal setting conditions

Physical: Psychological:

Appears to be associated with a deficit in the following skill area(s):

Statement of Need

Name:		Form:	Date:	Initials:

Objectives:

Skills to be extended:

New skills:

Strategies:

Outcomes and achievements:

Pupil Self Assessment Form

Name:...   Date:..

Teacher's Name:...........................   TA initials:....................................

Subject:..   Room:...

What were you doing at the time?			
The work was:.................... I felt:	Easy Happy	OK Bored	Hard Frustrated
	Too Little	Enough	Too much
Time to finish the task			
Time for your break			
Help from teacher			
Help from TA			
The other pupils were (tick the box)	helpful	annoying	distracting
Was the feedback from the teacher…?	praise	critical	helpful

Template 8.4

Behaviour Assessment Chart – to Discern Patterns and Outcomes of Behaviour

Name:................   Form:................   Date:................   Staff initials:................

Behaviour Outcomes	Week beginning:	Monday					Tuesday					Wednesday					Thursday					Friday				
	Periods	1	2	3	4	5	1	2	3	4	5	1	2	3	4	5	1	2	3	4	5	1	2	3	4	5
Teacher Initials																										
Support Staff Initials																										
Subject																										
Sensory Overload																										
Attention Seeking																										
Self-calm																										
Trying to exert control																										
Task Avoidance																										
Outside classroom/Transition (T)																										

Behaviour Outcomes	Week beginning:	Monday					Tuesday					Wednesday					Thursday					Friday				
	Periods	1	2	3	4	5	1	2	3	4	5	1	2	3	4	5	1	2	3	4	5	1	2	3	4	5
Teacher Initials																										
Support Staff Initials																										
Subject																										
Sensory Overload																										
Attention Seeking																										
Self-calm																										
Trying to exert control																										
Task Avoidance																										
Outside classroom/Transition (T)																										

Self-evaluation of practice

Self-evaluation is a natural part of the education process. Recognizing a mistake and the need to modify our own actions and behaviour is half way to solving the problem. This is especially true when working with pupils with AS, who may not react in the way you might expect.

Stereotyping pupils with a condition like autism is an easy trap to fall into. It is a common saying: 'If you've met one person with autism, you've met one person with autism.' They are individuals and vastly different from each other in their abilities, needs, the way they communicate, socialize, behave, process their environment and learn. Working with pupils with AS means that we have to come to the job with open minds, a willingness to learn, be flexible and adapt to their needs.

Assess the role we play when pupils with AS cannot manage their behaviour. Consider whether:

- We are part of the problem: for example, did not modify language; task was not broken down; insisted on eye contact; made pupil work in a group; or even being in a bad mood...
- Did not take action early enough: failed to remove pupil from classroom when showing signs of distress and/or sensory overload; did not prevent another pupil from being annoying to the pupil with AS.
- Failed to notice pupil struggling with task.
- Worsened the situation: interrupted the pupil with AS while they were talking; raised our voice.
- Made a mistake that caused a reaction with this particular pupil: wearing perfume; using a particular colour.

It is important to learn what we should *not* do with a particular child, as that will inform any action we might take.

Things to consider regarding one's own behaviour are:

- Did I modify my language?
- Was the task differentiated to meet the pupil's needs and enable them to complete the task?
- Did the pupil understand what was expected of him/her?
- Were there any sensory issues?
- Do I know the signs the pupil displays when getting distressed?
- If so, what was my response? Was it appropriate? Did it make the situation better or worse?

Pause for thought...

- What sort of mood am I in today – did this come across to the pupil?
- Do I know enough about ASCs to react appropriately to the pupil's needs?
- Do I know the characteristics of this pupil's ASC and their specific needs?
- Does this pupil trust me? Do I have a good relationship with this pupil? (This is very important with pupils with AS because they need to feel they are accepted and respected to feel safe and competent.)
- What can I do to ensure this does not reoccur?
- I can only change my actions. So, instead of getting angry, I can pause and give both of us some space. Work out a signal to use to let them know you are aware that you both need time out.

Discuss it with the pupil after the incident, when they are calm and rational. They may be able to help you understand the reasons for their behaviour and what would be a helpful way to respond which calms the situation and effects a better outcome in future. If the pupil is too young then speak to the parents. The parents will be encouraged that you are seeking to find a solution to help their child.

Contrary to popular belief, children with ASCs are very empathic. They pick up on a mood, nuance or atmosphere very quickly. They notice the smallest of clues, which tell the truth of the matter, due to detail focus processing. Their cool reaction in situations where you would expect a more emotional response is because they don't know what to do about it or what to say. It doesn't mean they don't feel things deeply; especially anything they feel is unjust or may humiliate them.

Meltdown

Tantrum	Meltdown	Signs of Approaching Meltdown
Goal driven.	Overwhelmed.	Zones out of their environment.
Checks to see if you are noticing.	Doesn't care whether you react or not.	Distraction – cannot concentrate.
Will take care not to get hurt.	No concern for their own or other's safety.	Muscle tension.
Calculating – will manipulate the social situation to their benefit.	No interest or awareness of the situation.	Can't speak coherently, stutters, echolalia, can't speak at all.
Will end when the goal is achieved or when situation resolved.	Meltdown will continue until it has run its course, nothing will stop it.	Attempts to block out sensory stimuli, e.g. covers ears, closes eyes, rocks.
Child in control.	Child not in control.	Clenches fists, jaw and may grind teeth.

A major concern for anyone who lives or works with a child with an ASC is the meltdown. Meltdown is not to be confused with a tantrum. It is a neurological response to stress and caused by the amygdala reflex, disordered processing and a chemical imbalance.

An older pupil can probably tell you what is likely to cause a meltdown and have some strategies to manage it, but the younger pupil will need considerable support to learn to manage meltdowns.

Meltdowns are more likely to happen when they are stressed. There will be clear warning signs. Find out from parents what the individual's 'Tell' signs are. These are physical indicators that alert you to their distress: a clenched fist, leg shaking, rocking, tense muscles.

Myles and Southwick outline three stages: Rumbling, Rage and Recovery. During the Rumbling stage there is the potential to avert a meltdown. Knowing your pupil's Tell signs is invaluable. The cues may be: body tension, fidgeting, grimacing, destroying their work, mumbling under their breath, calling out, refusing to do as they are told, a change in volume of their voice (up or down), tapping foot or hand.

If you are aware that a meltdown is imminent there are several things you can do:

● Discreetly acknowledge they are distressed by moving close to them, touching the fidgeting hand or leg (they must see this coming, and be aware that even a light touch may be physically painful).

- If the distress is caused by another pupil or even another adult, physically place yourself between your target pupil and that person, so that they cannot distract them.
- Direct their attention away from what is upsetting them.
- Use a sensory box with tactile objects that will calm the pupil.
- Distract them using their interest, humour, food and drink.
- When it becomes clear that the pupil has lost all concentration and is too distressed, remove them from the classroom to a quiet room.
- Engage them in a favourite activity that will distract or engage the senses and calm them. Use the sensory room.

In meltdown

The Rage stage can be very upsetting for all involved and may include physical violence against themselves, others or property. It may be emotional and loud or the pupil may withdraw and be unable to communicate at all.

Do not:
- Get into an argument with the pupil.
- Try to assert your authority.
- Issue threats.
- Raise your voice.
- Kettle them (trap them in a corner or lock them in a room).
- Use physical force unless it is to protect the pupil or others from harm.

Do avoid any provocation, which may make the situation worse.

Enabling the pupil to gain control is different from the adult controlling the situation. The former is achievable; the latter is not. Once a meltdown has started it has to run its course. Having lost all inhibition, at this stage they will not acknowledge rank nor reason.

So what do you do when a meltdown occurs?

Strategies for explosive situations

Elvén (2010) recommends strategies in stressful situations that may escalate into violent confrontation:

1 Step back away from them – reduce the threat by giving them space to calm down.
2 Walk away – do not engage in escalation of a situation, return when the pupil has calmed down.
3 Avoid eye contact – stay out of the pupil's line of vision.
4 Stop and listen to what the pupil has to say – do not argue with them.
5 Do not command or threaten – treat them as an equal and suggest a solution with an offer of help to support them succeed in making the right decision.
6 Offer two good choices – do you need time out for 10 or 15 minutes? Would you like to go to the library and read or to the playground and run around for 10 minutes?
7 Remember your goal is to help them regain control, not be in control of them.

Top Tip

Lead by example: if you want calm, be calm; if you want co-operation, listen and co-operate – negotiate a compromise.

Strategies for managing meltdowns

- Be prepared – know what strategies parents use when their child goes into meltdown.
- Stay calm. It is far more distressing for the person in meltdown than it is for you. They are totally overwhelmed.
- If you aren't the pupil's trusted key worker, send for them or someone else to support you discreetly, especially if the child is likely to flee.
- Other members of staff should not intervene, unless it is the key worker, who should take over and direct the Recovery period.
- If you can get to a quiet, familiar place, say 'Follow me' in a confident tone and go there.
- If you touch them lightly to attract their attention this may also distract them. Use your judgement in respect of the pupil you are with.
- Refusal to follow may be because the individual cannot process the instruction. They may not hear it.
- Sit to the side of the pupil, not opposite them, and wait quietly.
- If they curl up on the floor under a table or huddle in a corner and rock gently, let them.
- Do not stand over them in a threatening manner, march up and down the room, or criticize their behaviour.
- Some respond to calming techniques like, 'Close your eyes. Take a deep breath in, hold, breathe out; breathe in, hold, breathe out...' This may only work in a pre-meltdown stage, when they can still hear you.
- As you see them relax you might be able to help them regain control with a favourite pastime by putting a sketch pad, character cards, magazine or book within reach.
- Some meltdowns can be destructive – be prepared for this. Tony Attwood recommends having paper they can tear or plastic bottles to crush.
- In this situation calmly remove all unnecessary people from the room.
- If they run off, follow discreetly, at a distance, unless they are likely to leave the school premises and be at risk. In that situation, close the distance, explain why you need them to return to school in a calm voice and suggest a place they can be alone and safe.
- If you were the person with them at the outset, let another trusted member of staff step in and take over. The change of person may register and help calm down.
- When talking to someone in meltdown, use a low voice, speak slowly and clearly using as few words as possible. Avoid commenting on the incident.
- The pupil will be embarrassed. Acknowledge that you know they were upset and praise them for calming down.
- Avoid a patronizing tone but use short sentences so that they understand.

A meltdown can erupt out of nowhere or build up over the day. It can last for a few seconds or several minutes or longer. Remember a meltdown is a neurobiological response, not a tantrum.

Recovery and reflection

After they have calmed down, don't talk through the incident. Revisit it another time when the pupil is able to do so in a calm manner. They may not be able to recall what happened and it could trigger another meltdown if distressed further.

If they ask you 'Am I in trouble?' reassure them they are not.

Stay in the haven, allow them to calm down and get back into routine as soon as possible; send for class work if you do not feel it is appropriate to return to lessons. Use a subject of interest to motivate them. Ask the pupil, 'History now?'.

It is important to identify what triggered the meltdown and how they might manage the situation in future. If there were any witnesses, have them write an account of what they saw.

Consider the following:
- Medical problem – feeling unwell or sick? Check this first.
- The environment – space, noise levels, lighting or voice.
- People – attitudes, expectations, pair or group work, bullying.
- Teaching style – lecture, independent study, practicals, activity requiring self-organization, planning and execution of task, reading texts, criticism.
- Classwork – lack of understanding, lack of differentiation, too easy/too hard, revision, errors, time; homework.
- Sensory issues – wet clothes, smells, sounds, crowding.
- Change in routine – new teacher, different room, unexpected change in anything.

If there is a major issue with behaviour, discuss it with the SENCo and conduct an FBA. Comprehensive strategies for dealing with the behaviour should be applied universally and consistently by all staff to lessen the impact these distressing episodes have on the target pupil, their peers… the whole school.

Further reading

Smith Myles, B. and Southwick, J. (2005). *Asperger Syndrome and Difficult Moments: Practical solutions for tantrums, rage and meltdowns.* 2nd revised edition. Kansas: Autism Asperger Publishing Co.

Discipline and pupils with AS

Punishing pupils with AS is contentious because AS is a neuro-physiological disorder. 'Bad' behaviour may be a result of the condition. A meltdown is often when it occurs. In this state they rarely know what's happening or what they are doing. It can be frightening. They may kick a door so hard it breaks, lash out at another pupil, or throw a chair across a room. It's distressing for everybody, especially the pupil with AS, who may not be conscious of what is happening until it is all over.

Establish the cause. If it is a sensory overload, disciplining the pupil is inappropriate; schools need to take responsibility to meet the needs of pupils with AS. If it was frustration, for example, and the pupil rejects help and goes into meltdown, then there should be consequences. Autism explains the behaviour but does not excuse it.

What those consequences should be is another matter. Are consequences punishment or outcomes? Often the pupil with AS does not react to punishment in the way we would expect. Punishment is often used as a deterrent but this is only effective if the pupil knows what will happen if they do something and the punishment is something they don't want to do. To be sent out of a noisy lesson is not really a punishment for a pupil who is experiencing sensory overload or sees the lesson as being pointless. Also every occasion is perceived as a unique experience so the pupil may not learn the 'lesson' and behave better next time because no two experiences are necessarily the same, although you may see it that way if the same 'bad behaviour' occurs again in the same subject, same room and with the same teacher. It may be a sunny day on the first occasion and a rainy day the next, so in the autistic mind it is completely different.

The Colour Wheel

One way to prevent meltdown is to enable the child to recognize the different stages leading up to it. Teach the young pupil to associate the different stages with feelings using the Colour Wheel, a circle with quarters in different colours that relate to the four stages:

1 Calm and content – safe and able to do what is asked.
2 Anxious and getting upset – confused and worried.
3 Angry and frightened – distressed by others' behaviour or fear of failure.
4 Panic and meltdown – out of control, may be self-injurious and violent.

- Colour in the wheel with conventional colours: green, yellow, orange and red, or discuss with pupil which colour best reflects how they feel; or even use shapes: flat for calm, undulating for anxious, angry spikes and lightning bolts for meltdown.
- Discuss how they feel in relation to the colours or shapes.
- Put pictures of things that trigger these feelings in the outer circle.
- Use a Comic Conversation (Carol Gray) to help the pupil recognize what they feel and do when they are beginning to feel anxious.
- Identify what strategies they can use to avoid getting more upset and head into the next zone.
- Use the Comic Conversation to identify the point at which they have a choice, while they can still make it, in the yellow or orange zones; yellow to start with young pupils – orange may be too late.
- Illustrate the outcomes of the good choice and the bad choice.
- Give them the tools to make the good choice. Use traffic lights to signal they need help; a booklet of a favourite interest: dinosaurs, trains, My Little Pony; sensory box. Be guided by the child and the parents to ensure you have the best tools for the pupil.
- Using social stories incorporating visual aids to teach them what to do when they feel anxious. Use 'What if' key fobs.

Template 8.5

My Colour Wheel of Feelings

Name: ....

Class: ....

Teacher/TA: ....

Anxious

Angry

Calm

Meltdown

Punishment v Learning Self-Discipline

In school punishments are reactive: the pupil does something the teacher finds objectionable, therefore the teacher decides to punish them. The punishment is then decided on the spot and handed out, usually a detention during lunch, break or after school, or internal exclusion.

I have asked pupils in the internal exclusion room why they thought they were being excluded from lessons. Rarely was it understood as being a punishment for unacceptable behaviour. As such, it is ineffective and will not be a deterrent.

The child with AS generally won't do things out of badness. That doesn't mean to say that they don't do bad things – but their motivation for doing them is different. Their inability to predict what is going to happen next with any reasonable accuracy creates anxiety, distress and fear. At these times the need to control the situation may be overwhelming. Under these circumstances, a pupil with AS may reason: if I do this then teacher will do that... and derive some comfort from knowing what will happen. The problem arises when it is bad behaviour causing the teacher to shout and reprimand the pupil. Without understanding the motives behind the action, we make the assumption that the pupil is deliberately behaving badly, being rude or manipulative rather than anxious or distressed, especially when the pupil smiles in relief upon achieving the desired reaction, interpreted as smirking.

When they have calmed down, ask them to tell you what happened. They will usually tell the truth even if it shows them to be wrong. However, they may be too distressed to do this the same day. Older children may find it easier to write it down; younger children may find a Comic Conversation helpful and you draw the incident.

Their version of what happened may be enlightening. Do not dismiss a totally outlandish explanation as a pack of lies. Remember that the way the pupil with AS perceives the world is completely different from yours. He may see the behaviour as perfectly logical.

What next? Exclusion is the conventional approach. Is it the most effective? The pupil needs to learn what is inappropriate behaviour and how to exercise self-discipline.

Once a decision has been made, there should be consequences for their actions. An intervention is more effective than punishment. Tell them when the intervention is going to take place, where and with whom. The pupil's key worker, with whom they have a good relationship and trust, is the ideal person.

An Extraordinary Letter of Apology

An Extraordinary Letter of Apology is a strategy designed to help older pupils with AS:

- Recognize the bad behaviour.
- Acknowledge the effect their actions have on others.
- Suggest appropriate alternatives.

Having autism makes it difficult for someone with AS to imagine these – we need to teach them.

- When? When they have calmed down, the next day or later.
- Where? If applying sanctions – internal exclusion room, otherwise a quiet room.
- Who with? Key worker – someone they trust.

Resources:

- Witness account of the incident – a scrupulously accurate narrative.
- Paper.
- Pens – including red, green, orange and blue.

1   Read the account.
2   Pupil to underline in green when someone tried to help, for example by asking 'Would you like time out?', or picking up something they threw down.
3   In red, underline when they behaved badly, for example spoke rudely or threw something.
4   Check every incident is acknowledged.
5   Discuss each point with the pupil, asking: Why was that the wrong thing to do? How do you think this made them feel? How would you feel if…?
6   During this stage they usually realize they have behaved badly and apologise. Reassure them. Say, 'We're going to write a letter together to say sorry to….'
7   Go through the account with the orange pen and draw an arrow at a place when an alternative presents itself and write in blue what they could have done instead, for example walked away.
8   The pupil writes the letter including: acknowledgements of what they did wrong; why it was wrong; how they made the other person feel; and what they could have done instead.
9   Deliver the letter and wait for the apology to be acknowledged.
10 The person receiving the apology should simply thank them.
11 Do not reprimand them or extract a promise not to repeat the behaviour.
12 Do not mention the incident again unless they do or you are praising them for their understanding and apology.

Further reading

Gray, C. (1994). *Comic Strip Conversations: Illustrated interactions that teach conversation skills to students with autism and related disorders*. Texas: Future Horizons.

Exclusion

Excluding a child with an ASC is becoming a major issue. Informal exclusions are not only against the spirit of inclusion, but illegal when schools exclude children from school trips, during inspections, or children are simply sent home early after an incident. There is also a serious concern that some schools are failing to make reasonable adjustments that enable these children to learn, and there are too many losing out on their education.

Research carried out in 2014 by Ambitious About Autism suggests that 40 per cent of children with autism had been informally excluded from schools and 20 per cent were formally excluded. Based on these figures they concluded that 28,000 children might have been illegally excluded from education, with reports of short days and early 'pick ups' from school (BBC, 11 February 2014).

Parents are becoming increasingly aware of their children's rights under the Education, SEN, Equality and Human Rights laws. There are a number of support groups such as the NAS, Ambitious About Autism and IPSEA (Independent Parental Special Education Advice), advising parents about the proper procedures for excluding children and they are more prepared to take action against schools who fail to observe these and engage in other dubious exclusion practices.

9　Bullying and Asperger Syndrome

Over 40 per cent of children on the autistic spectrum have been bullied at school. The impact on children and families can be devastating. Many of the children and families we surveyed report damage to self-esteem, mental health and progress at school. Some withdraw from school altogether, others never fully recover from their experiences.

B. Reid and A. Batten (2006)

The impact of bullying as mentioned above cannot be ignored, as the personal cost to the individual being bullied and their families, and the financial cost to services is huge. Bullying takes place in all schools; what they do about it is what matters.

Why is the pupil with AS a target for bullies?

First we need to understand why, out of all the population, being a victim of bullying has such a devastating impact upon the individual with AS. A child's innocence, taking everything at face value, remains with autistic people into adulthood, unless they are taught and able to analyse behaviour. They have no defence mechanisms against bullying – they are confused, trying to understand why a person would wish to make fun of their interests or behaviour; set them up; lie to them; steal from them; or cheat. A strong sense of justice and fairness is a common trait in autism. If you lie to them they will feel betrayed and remember it for a very long time.... Why wouldn't they? A child will wait until the exact time you have assured them you will do something; if a person says they will do something at a certain time then there is the expectation that they will do that then. Why wouldn't they? How often have parents told you that their child will wait until the exact time they have been assured they will do something, and fallen apart when it doesn't happen at the precise time agreed? If you make a 'promise' to a child with autism you must fulfil that promise.

The AS child and bullying

● Communication difficulties make it impossible to figure out what is hidden behind teasing; they understand, only too well, when people laugh at them but why do they mock them in this way? This confusion often reduces them to tears of frustration and they simply do not know what to do.

　I have seen older children with AS reduced to tears in these situations, which, in our society, is not age appropriate and leaves them open to further peer ridicule.

- The lack of social imagination makes it difficult for them to predict what the other person's intentions are and this is often misinterpreted. Having only their own limited experience and imagination to decode what is happening, they may imagine that the other person thinks as they do, when nothing could be further from the truth. The realization that someone is mocking them or trying to set them up and hurt their feelings is shattering.
- The inability of the child to report bullying through lack of understanding and fear means that it can continue for a long time before anyone realizes what is happening. The child will withdraw and their behaviour will become more erratic – hiding under furniture or in dark places. The child will refuse to go to school, become more attached to their parents, their sleep will be disturbed, they often have nightmares and their eating becomes sporadic.
- More attention needs to be paid to the social interactions of these pupils.

Why a target?

- AS is a hidden condition.
- Obsessive interests, which are often not age appropriate. In primary school the child who knows the Latin names of dinosaurs and has encyclopaedic knowledge of the topic will stand out.
- Idiosyncratic behaviours, rituals and stims.
- Monotonous tone, odd speech patterns, advanced vocabulary, over-politeness and old-fashioned ways of expressing themselves.
- Literal interpretation of language.
- Apparent lack of humour.
- Inability to read social cues and making social errors all the time.
- Self-isolation.
- Sensory sensitivities.
- The inability to communicate to staff that they are being bullied through poor working memory, the time it takes to process an incident, or the lack of ability to express themselves.

All these make the pupil with AS very vulnerable and, therefore, our reaction to the pupil who is a victim of bullying has to take into account their vulnerability. We cannot tell children with AS to toughen up or ignore it: they have to be given the tools to fight back.

Because AS is a hidden condition and largely to do with social interaction and behaviour, there is a tendency towards a lack of understanding and tolerance to the way AS shows itself. The child will be labelled rude and badly behaved. Autism awareness is vital if the child is to be accepted in society, and the first experience a child gets of the bigger society is in a school. Everyone in the school should be made aware of the impact autism has upon an individual.

Bullying a pupil with AS affects their self-esteem, mental well-being, development of social skills and any academic progress they might make in school. Of great concern is that the individual with AS will come to believe that the way they are treated is all they deserve, because they are worthless. The confusion surrounding this treatment makes them easy targets. They are unable to understand what is really happening: that they are being set up, and even after the event they will return to attempt to befriend the bullies because they are the only people who bother about them or talk to them. They do not understand what a real friend is. A very superficial relationship can become very important.

The after-effects of bullying go on to ruin the lives of some victims; leading to problems with low self-esteem, further isolation, depression, fear and mental illness. They replay the event in their mind over and over again, feeling the same emotions of confusion, humiliation, impotence and despair as they did when it took place. This can lead to self-harm and suicide.

Pupils with AS generally want to make friends but lack the necessary social and communication skills and may exhibit odd behaviours, which make it difficult for them to become accepted by their peers, and this odd behaviour attracts unwanted attention. Some of the behaviours of a pupil with AS attempting to interact may be misunderstood and seen as bullying or harassment. A thoughtful gesture or kind remark made to a pupil with AS may lead them to believe they have found a friend. This 'friend' may then find themself being followed around the playground. Attention-seeking behaviour may be aggressive, such as pulling clothing or parts of the body. There may be a lack of awareness of personal space and the pupil with AS may go right up to another child, putting their face very close to theirs while talking, especially if seeking that person's attention.

Socially naive and, without a group of friends to support them, they are easy victims.

Are you doing the most you can?

The following is an extract from research conducted by Symes and Humphrey (2011):

> Robertson, Chamberlain & Kasari (2003) found that the more negative relationship teachers had with such pupils, the less socially accepted they were by their peers. This is particularly worrying as the difficulties in social interaction experienced by pupils with ASDs already put them at risk of negative social outcomes.

There is anecdotal evidence of teachers and TAs ignoring teasing and bullying, and even condoning it by suggesting the victim ignores the teasing 'walk away and it will go away' or that the victim should 'toughen up'. This strategy does not stop teasing and may, in fact, encourage the bullies to escalate the 'teasing' so that it becomes bullying. People may even blame the victim for the bullying, saying that they brought it on themselves. Inappropriate action is common, for example removing the victim from the classroom and teaching them in isolation, while the perpetrators continue to be taught in class.

The use of sarcasm is likely to be taken literally and may lead to great upset. Avoid it in conversation with your target pupil with AS or even with the class they are part of. Teachers may be unaware of the devastating effect it has on pupils with AS; if this is the case, please warn them that the pupil may be confused, feel stupid and targeted, having a perception that they are being bullied. It may have a lasting effect on their self-esteem, which will impact on their ability to learn.

Pupils with AS may not report instances of bullying, which can lead to an escalation in the bullying they suffer. Or they may report every incident of teasing or being knocked accidentally when going from one lesson to the next in crowded corridors, and be regarded as the child who cried 'Wolf!'.

The positive attitudes of TAs working with pupils with AS is crucial to their inclusion as valued members of the school community. When working as a TA supporting pupils with AS, I was always keen to show how much I enjoyed my interaction with them. It wasn't difficult. They are remarkable individuals. Staff in primary schools are role models for young children and, as such, have a responsibility to act immediately to counter the bullying and show understanding and tolerance of behaviours associated with the condition.

However, there are two parts to the problem: 1) identifying the 'teasing' or 'bullying' as being malicious and 2) neutralizing it. A pupil with AS has problems assessing verbal bullying because of their tendency to take things literally, and they will need to be taught the difference between banter and malicious bullying intended to humiliate.

Strategies for the pupil

- Teach the pupil what bullying is. Laminate the Am I Being Bullied 'questions'. Put them on a key fob for the pupil, who can use them to assess whether they were bullied.
- Ensure the pupil understands that:
  - they are not alone, and
  - it is not their fault.
  - No-one has the right to treat them like that.
- Encourage them to report any instances of bullying during Social Skills lessons.
- Teach the pupil one liners (fogging) to say in response to verbal teasing (see below for suggestions).
- Ensure the pupil is not left unsupervised in areas of risk – PE changing room, toilets and the playground at break times.
- Make the disabled toilets available to them to change in and use.
- Encourage retreating to the Haven when feeling threatened.
- Initiate lunchtime clubs in the pupil's area of interest: for example, chess or manga drawing. The pupil could take the lead and teach others.
- Hold an Autism Awareness Assembly with the whole school.
- Set up a Buddy System within the form with peers who want to help support the pupil with AS to get through the day, especially at break times.
- Pupil Mentors with high status could spend time once a week with the younger pupil with AS.
- Use Drama to highlight problems with bullying.
- Use Drama to develop skills to combat bullying.
- Empower bystanders to intervene.
- Have a bully box in the school where bullying can be reported discretely.

Strategies for staff

- Awareness of the types of bullying that go on among young people, including backhanded bullying (being deceived into doing something inappropriate), cyber-bullying and hazing. (Hazing is ritual humiliation, which is endured in order to be accepted into a group.)
- Zero tolerance of bullying.
- Be patient and listen.
- Take every report of bullying seriously and investigate it.
- Never punish the pupil for behaviour related to their autism.
- Do not use sarcasm and avoid teasing.
- Play to the pupil's strengths in class.
- Read books about autism, as recommended by the NAS; they are all available on Amazon:

Ages 3 – 5 years

Gorrod, L. (1997). *My Brother is Different*. London: NAS.

Hannah, L. (2007). *My friend Sam: introducing a child with autism to a nursery school*. London: NAS.

Hunter, S.T. (2006). *My Sister is Different*. London: NAS.

Lears, L. (2003). *Ian's Walk: a story about autism*. Morton Grove, IL: Albert Whitman & Co.

Ages 5 – 8 years

Brock, C. (2007). *My Family is Different*. London: NAS.

Shally, C. (2007). *Since We're Friends: an autism picture book*. Centerton, AR: Awaken Specialty Press.

Van Niekerk, C. and Venter, L. (2006). *Understanding Sam and Asperger Syndrome*. Erie, PA: Skeezel Press.

Ages 6 – 11 years

Barraclough, S. (2012). *I Know Someone with Autism*. Oxford: Raintree.

Murrell, D. (2007). *Friends learn about Tobin*. Arlington, TX: Future Horizons.

Ogaz, N. (2002). *Buster and the Amazing Daisy: adventures with Asperger syndrome*. London: Jessica Kingsley Publishers.

Powell, J. (2006). *Thomas has autism*. London: Evans Brothers.

Ages 9 – 13 years

Birch, S. (2009). *Dead Puzzling*.YouWriteOn.com

Boyd, B. (2007). *Asperger Syndrome, the swan and the burglar*. Milton Keynes: Author House.

Dowd, S. (2008). *The London Eye Mystery*. London: David Fickling.

Haldane, C. and Jones, K. (2008). *Dannie's dilemma*. London: Chipmunka. Also available: *Dannie's Dilemma: Book Two: the spelling saga*

Hoopman, K. (2001). *Blue Bottle Mystery: an Asperger mystery*. London: Jessica Kingsley Publishers.

Skye, L. (2012). *The Adventures of Maisie Voyager*. London: Jessica Kingsley Publishers.

Watts, G. (2012). *Kevin thinks …about outer space, confusing expressions and the perfectly logical world of Asperger syndrome*. London: Jessica Kingsley Publishers.

- Read Dubin's and/or Heinrichs' books!

Further reading

Dubin, N. (2007). *Asperger Syndrome and Bullying Strategies and Solutions*. London: Jessica Kingsley Publishers.

Heinrichs, R. (2003). *Perfect Targets: Asperger syndrome and bullying – practical solutions for surviving the social world*. Kansas: Autism Asperger Publishing Co.

Reid, B. and Batten, A. (2006). *B is for Bullied: the experience of children with autism and their families*. London: NAS.

Stobart, A. (2009). *Bullying and Autism Spectrum Disorders: a guide for school staff*. London: NAS.

Am I being bullied?

Am I hurt?

Call me nasty names?

Lying about me?

Stop me playing?

Don't listen when I talk?

More than 2 times?

Want to hurt me?

Was I scared?

Laugh at me?

Feelings I have because I am Being Bullied?

No friends.

I feel stupid.

I hurt.

I feel bad.

I'm scared.

I feel sick.

I don't want to eat.

I don't want to go to school.

I can't sleep.

I have bad dreams.

No-one listens.

Hit something.

Angry.

I don't know what to do.

Hurt myself.

Run away.

Tell teacher.

Tell mum or dad.

Tell me.

Safe place.

Tell a friend.

Leave me alone!

No!

Go away!

Get away from them.

Go to.

Peer interventions to combat bullying

The following are ideas for interventions to support pupils with AS in mainstream schools when they were having problems making friends.

If the authority has an Autism Outreach Team, I recommend that you contact them to advise you and help devise and/or lead any peer intervention strategies.

Autism Awareness Assembly

This can be a very effective intervention but it must explain:

- 'Why' the pupil with AS is different: brain development, and
- 'How' this affects the behaviour of the person on the autism spectrum.
- The special qualities of individuals with AS and positive role models.

This has to be done in a way that your audience understands, and that could be a challenge, so if you do not have a specialist in the school, I recommend that you invite the Autism Outreach team from your local council or a private speaker on the subject.

Circle of Friends

The Circle of Friends is a strategy that is very effective in providing peer support for children who have difficulties because of their autism. It must be very carefully set up and managed by a lead professional – teaching assistant or teacher. A group of pupils who are likely to be supportive of the autism pupil are asked to volunteer to be the focus pupil's circle of friends. The group meets every week to discuss ways they can support the focus pupil to develop their interaction skills, sharing what worked well for the pupil and what targets to set for the following week. Before initiating a Circle of Friends it is important to set it up correctly and go through all the stages as set out in the Leicestershire Autism Outreach Team programme which can be found online here: http://www.leics.gov.uk/autism_circle_of_friends.pdf.

Circle of Friends is also outlined on the NAS website here: http://www.autism.org.uk/working-with/education/educational-professionals-in-schools/resources-for-teachers/circle-of-friends-promoting-inclusion-and-interaction.aspx.

Buddy System

This is a tried and tested model of inclusive practice to encourage the integration of pupils with difficulties into the school community, but it is a strategy better suited for an intervention with older pupils or those who have been on the Circle of Friends programme but are ready to go it alone without regular meetings. This also has to be dealt with sensitively. The Buddies will not only have to be responsible members of the school community with high status, but also those who will be able to understand the particular difficulties associated with autism, tolerant of the way the pupil behaves, and mindful of the fact that the pupil with AS may become very reliant upon the 'friendship'. The pupil will have to be taught the social conventions of the peer group. It is not enough to trust that they will be able to observe and imitate. I recommend a group of Buddies from the pupil's class or a senior member of the school on a sports team if the pupil has an interest in a particular sport.

Often pupils with AS have a special interest or skill that can be built up by setting up a club around the interest and encouraging the pupil to lead the group. Examples include: chess, music, drama, video gaming, raspberry pi, manga and war gaming.

If the pupil can lead the group and teach the skill it will help elevate the pupil's status and raise self-esteem. It will have to be monitored because the communication and social skills of the pupil with AS may be impaired and misunderstood.

Class project: Positive role models who may have had AS

Anecdotal accounts in diaries and letters and considered observations of contemporary behaviour have led to a number of well-known figures being identified as probably having the condition. An Aspie hero board, featuring different adults who have been successful in their field, could be displayed and changed every week, as a positive message.

Do some research. Take opportunities to relate a lesson to a person with autism in a positive way.

There are also the fictional characters from children's favourite programmes: Sherlock Holmes, Dr Who, Spock and Data from Star Trek.

Strategy

As a class project you could choose to explore the life and work of an Aspie Hero. 'People who have changed the world?' Do not tell them at this stage that this person may have been autistic.

Task:
1 Pupils do the biography, researching the person's later achievements.
2 If possible, teacher researches how the subject was viewed as a child, as well as a difficult adult, if possible; many would have been regarded as obsessive, stupid, lazy, weird... and

You need to find the right person – here are some suggestions:

Joy Adamson	Woody Allen	Hans Christian Andersen
W. H. Auden	Isaac Asimov	Dan Ackroyd
Ludwig van Beethoven	Alexander Bell	Pip Brown/Ladyhawke
David Bellamy	Tim Burton	Arthur C. Clarke
Lewis Carroll	Marie Curie	Leonardo da Vinci
Charles Darwin	Arthur Conan Doyle	Bob Dylan
Thomas Edison	Albert Einstein	Bobby Fischer
Henry Ford	Dian Fossey	Bill Gates
Antoni Gaudi	Darryl Hannah	Jim Henson
Alfred Hitchcock	Thomas Jefferson	Wassily Kandinsky
L. S. Lowry	Michelangelo	Mozart
Isaac Newton	Gary Numan	George Orwell
Michael Palin	Carl Sagan	George Bernard Shaw
Steven Spielberg	Satoshi Tajiri	Daniel Tammet
James Taylor	Nikola Tesla	Alan Turing
Mark Twain	Vincent van Gogh	Andy Warhol
George Washington		

These are all people who have achieved remarkable things in their field of interest. If you do a lesson on one of the above, mention that they may have been autistic; this will reinforce a positive message about autism.

Discuss their achievements. People with Asperger's Syndrome are born with a different way of seeing the world. It's not better ... not worse ... just different.

Sometimes 'autistic characteristics' can make a real difference. After the presentation, ask the pupils if they think 'the character' has changed the world for the rest of us and to give their reasons for their opinion.

Don't emphasize the idea of 'genius', rather draw attention to the fact that with Asperger's Syndrome it is possible to concentrate on something for a really long period of time. Why would being able to focus on something be a good thing?

They have the imagination to create inventions or ideas and solutions to problems, amazing works of art and music which require so much time that the rest of us would be bored, dismayed and ready to give up.

Here are some examples of how 'interests' and perseverance have led to great achievements.

- Michelangelo took 4 years to paint the ceiling of the Sistine Chapel, from start to finish. He was absent for at least two long periods during that time but went on to paint the 'Last Judgement', which took 6 years.
- Spielberg made his first film for his photography badge as a boy scout, age 12, but only achieved success in 1974 with *Jaws*. Since then he has directed many films that you all know. He likes to spend his free time watching films back to back.
- Charles Darwin's father told him when he was 16, 'You care for nothing but shooting, dogs and rat-catching, and you will be a disgrace to yourself and all your family.' He studied to be a clergyman but his hobby was natural history, especially beetles. He set out on HMS *Beagle* 1831-1836 and published *On the Origin of Species* in 1859!
- Marie Curie and her husband Pierre announced the existence of radium in 1898. In 1910 Marie Curie, working on without her husband, who had been killed in 1906, isolated 10 grams of pure radium metal after processing tons of pitch blend.
- Savants: 'savant' comes from the French word 'savoir', meaning to know. Savants are people with a learning disability who have pools of extraordinary ability, like the artist Stephen Wiltshire and Derek Paravacini, the blind pianist. One in ten people with autism have some ability and 10 per cent of savants are people with autism. However, 'prodigious savants', like Daniel Tammet, mathematician, multi-linguist and author, who has Asperger Syndrome, are extremely rare. There are less than 100 such people in the whole world!

Luke Jackson said with regard to television programmes about savants,

I find these television programs (sic) depressing, I got all the nerdiness and freakishness but none of the genius.

However, it has been my experience that many younger pupils with AS are proud to be associated with them and see them as genuine role models.

There are several videos about these savants on YouTube, which you might use in an assembly or intervention:

Derek Paravacini: Musical Genius
Daniel Tammet: The Boy with the Incredible Brain
Stephen Wiltshire draws a picture of Rome in 3 days: Beautiful Minds

Peer Intervention

There are a number of reasons why you might think it is a good idea to do a Peer Intervention on behalf of a pupil with AS. It may be part of the good autism practice that the school undertakes towards inclusion. Another reason may be that the pupil wants to tell their peers that they have Asperger Syndrome and explain their behaviour, because they are aware of the impact their idiosyncrasies have on their desire to make friends and be accepted for who they are.

The other motivation for a Reactive Peer Intervention may be that staff have witnessed that the relationship between the pupil with AS and their peers is deteriorating at such a rate, because of their odd behaviour, that they are in danger of being totally ostracized and isolated by their peers and this may lead to bullying. This is to be avoided at all costs because the impact on the self-esteem of the pupil can lead to a negative effect on their academic achievement and, at the very worst, tragic consequences.

However, this has to be dealt with very sensitively with regard to the feelings of both the pupil with AS and their parents. Many parents do not want it known that their child has an autism spectrum condition and you must respect their wishes. Their motivation is that they fear for their child and the attention they might attract from it being generally known they are on the spectrum. Some parents, who acknowledge that they are on the spectrum themselves, may have had terrible experiences at school and therefore this has to be a joint undertaking.

If the school initiates the intervention it needs to be discussed between the key TA and the form tutor. They may be able to highlight where any issues might arise around the pupil and their peers. Do not mention it to the pupil before speaking to the parents. Remember that some pupils may be unaware they have autism. Invite the parents in to discuss the intervention and explain why you consider it to be necessary.

Once you have the agreement of the parents, tell them what you intend to do and how. Invite them to help their child put the presentation together. Go through your contribution to the presentation with the parents so that they understand exactly what you are going to do and are reassured that this is not going to humiliate their son or daughter. I do not recommend that parents attend the intervention with the class. The pupil may be very anxious and this may add to their distress. Reassure the pupil that they have the right to withdraw from their part in the intervention and that you will support them every moment during the talk.

If there is another pupil with AS, who has done this before and would like to help, invite them to give advice and support. It will reassure the pupil giving the talk and also raise the self-esteem of both pupils.

Asperger Syndrome and me: Peer Intervention Strategy

1   Keep the format simple – a PowerPoint presentation is helpful because it allows photographs to be used to illustrate the 'text'.
2   Split the presentation into two parts: the pupil and the condition.
3   **Part I:** the pupil with AS gives a talk about themselves to their form, introducing themselves:
   a   My name is *****.
   b   I have a sister/brother who is a pain… (usually), a dog and a cat.
   c   My interests are … military history and restoring old minis. Here is a photo of me with my dad at a mini rally at Goodwood, last year. It took us 2 years to put this car back together!
   d   The best holiday I had was… because…

e   My favourite subjects are...

f   And finally: My name is ***** and I have Asperger Syndrome. I have a different operating system and sometimes I need help with....

4   The idea is that they are just kids with similar interests to everyone else but...

5   **Part 2:** adult explains what Asperger Syndrome is: a difference in the way the brain is formed (use the net diagrams in this book) and the way it works.

6   Explain how this can lead to difficulties in communication and misunderstanding.

7   There are two main areas of behaviour to explain – lack of inhibition and sensory overload.

8   Option – show videos from YouTube (see below).

9   Finally, mention some of the more gifted people with AS, like Bill Gates and Steve Jobs, that the peers can relate to and point out that while it's difficult in school – people like ***** could change the world.

10 Ask for the peers to help provide support for the pupil during the school day, and explain the Buddy system.

Websites

NAS http://www.autism.org.uk/working-with/education/educational-professionals-in-schools/resources-for-teachers/bullying-and-autism-spectrum-disorders-a-guide-for-school-staff.aspx

Cartoon – what to do if you are being bullied – http://www.cyh.com/HealthTopics/HealthTopicDetailsKids.aspx?p=335&np=290&id=1572

Bullied – what to do if you are being bullied for children age 4-6 – http://www.gosh.nhs.uk/children/general-health-advice/cartoons/bullying/

Videos

A short video about Ben's Circle of Friends can be found on the TES resources website here: http://www.tes.co.uk/teaching-resource/Teachers-TV-Circle-of-Friends-Ben-6048743/

BBC Newsround – My Autism and Me: Rosie here: http://www.youtube.com/watch?v=ejpWWP1HNGQ

Part Three

Part Three

10   Organization – practicalities

The super-organized individual with AS may insist on everything being in its right place as a way of controlling their environment. Let them organize their workspace as they want. It is a discreet ritual and preventing it may cause distress.

They may be utterly hopeless at organization, leaving their things all over the school then getting anxious because they can't find anything and will get into trouble. Be very patient and reassuring. Helping the pupils with AS organize themselves at school is one of the key tasks because it reduces levels of anxiety.

Before the pupil arrives in school, the routine from getting them out of bed to going to school may be conducted with military precision. It is likely that they will have to be reminded to do basic things every day. They may be highly 'organized' at home with instructions displayed, telling them what to do to prepare for the day: how to wash, which clothes to wear, what things to put in their schoolbag. Parents may use visual symbols to reinforce the message.

Communicate in Print 2 (Widgit) may appear to be childish and patronizing; however, it is an internationally recognized resource used to support communication in a variety of situations. On websites like the Autism Education Trust, if you run the cursor along the text it will automatically add the illustrations to clarify what is being said.

Top Tip

Never criticize the pupil with AS for their difficulties with organization. It won't change anything, just lower their self-esteem. Put strategies in place to help them.

Strategies

- Establish routines for arriving in school, lesson preparation, assembly... Use language jigs or key fobs, that the pupil can see or carry, to support this.
- Colour code the visual timetable – match the colour of subject to the colour of the exercise books used in that subject.
- Colour code the tools used and assign the pupil a colour.
- Fill in the homework diary using the same subject colour codes, highlighting when the homework must be done and when it must be handed in.
- Symbols may be used to illustrate subjects and instructions, for example, an open book for doing the homework and a closed one for handing it in.
- Attach a Velcro strip to the table in front of the pupil. Stick visual cue cards for each activity on the strip in the order they will be done in the lesson. Task completed: remove activity card.

- Include reward activity cards to encourage the pupil to complete the task.
- Place all the tools the pupil needs for the lesson in a tray or box with their name or photo on the front.
- Put an illustrated checklist of equipment required for the lesson on a key fob for easy reference, or use a large work mat with illustrations around the perimeter so that they can do their work in the middle.
- Develop this skill using the Practical 1 template (see below) to help the pupil focus on how to organize.
- Give the pupil an illustrated checklist and a tray to collect the tools.
- Pupil selects the pictures of the equipment they need for the lesson, then puts them in a tray.
- Arrange for PE gear to be put somewhere safe at the beginning of the day and return it to the same place at the end of the lesson.
- Remind the pupil to take the kit home to be washed at regular intervals.
- Include all equipment necessary for what they are learning in PE: mouth guard, shin pads, gloves… and support with images if necessary.
- Note any regular after school clubs supported with appropriate symbols denoting the activity, be it sport, drama or music…

Template 10.1 – Practical 1

Subject: ....

Task: I have to ....

....

....

....

I need: ....

....

....

....

I am going to: ....

....

....

I found: ....

....

....

....

Template 10.2 – Key Fobs

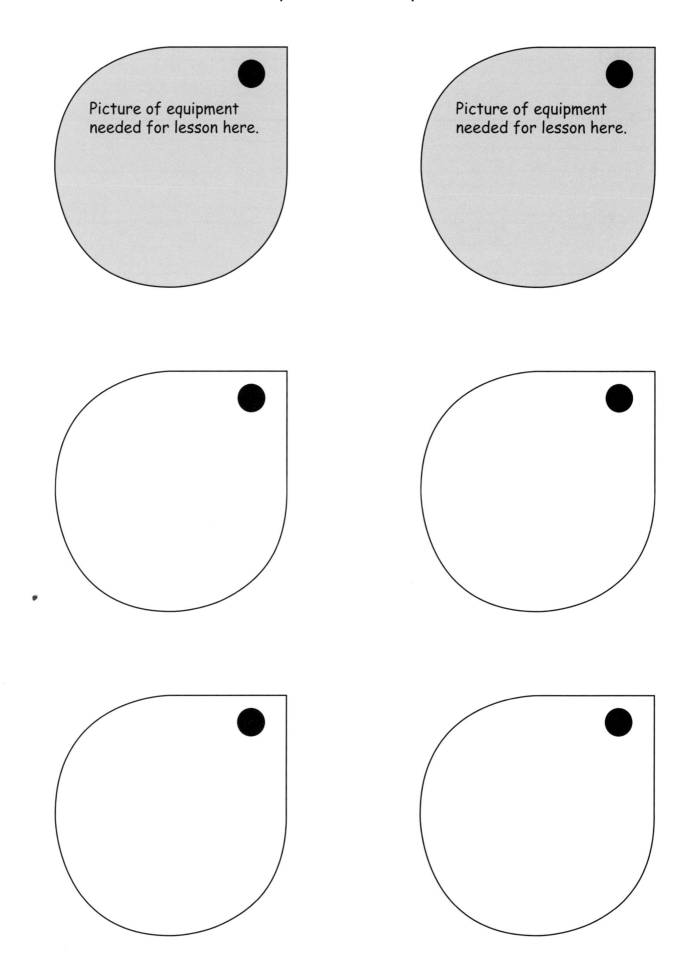

Picture of equipment needed for lesson here.

Picture of equipment needed for lesson here.

Websites

Communicate in Print 2 – http://www.widgit.com/products/inprint/index.htm

Questions to ask when supporting the pupil with AS to organize their eork

- 'What did Mrs Collins tell you to do?'
- 'What things will you need?'
- 'What will you do first?'
- 'What will you do after that?'
- 'What will you do when you have finished?'

Don't ask the next question until you have received an answer to the previous one, and allow time for processing.

You could write the questions down on a key fob. Break it down to one task per fob. After a while the pupil may learn what to do without prompting, but it will take time.

Top Tip

Do not alter the wording of your question. Repeat it again, after a suitable interval, using exactly the same words.

11 Autism is a communication difficulty

Communication is around 20 per cent verbal and 80 per cent body language. Add to that the ability to understand the intention of the speaker, or being able to 'read between the lines', and you begin to understand the level of skill required to communicate. This is a set of skills people with an ASC have to be taught carefully and repeatedly, and may never use effectively.

Cognition is the mental action or process of acquiring knowledge and understanding through thought, experience, and the senses. Cognitive processing is a much bigger challenge for pupils with AS than we appreciate. Research has shown that people with autism have to harness an extra area of the brain to try and make sense of things we take for granted. It's hard work. By the end of the day the pupil may be exhausted.

Another problem may be the inability to retain information that has just been given and relate it to the task set. NT brains can hold information that is not required at that moment but which they will need later during the task. When needed, it is retrieved effortlessly. This is called a working memory. The brain of someone with AS will struggle to recall what they need, where it should go, or in which order.

Top Tip

Write the task down (with illustrations/symbols) one step at a time. Use numbering and/or the key fob template to maintain the order of the task. Use the least number of words possible.

Literacy and Maths

It is a popular myth that all pupils with AS are brilliant at maths. However, the English component of the questions can be particularly confusing. Modern maths requires a high level of literacy and knowledge of mathematical vocabulary. However, if a pupil shows an aptitude beyond their years for maths, science or any other subject, develop it. Discuss this with your SENCo. Suggest getting in a specialist tutor. Developing a skill or an interest in this way will encourage pupils to have a positive experience in schools.

Language in maths can cause major difficulties because many of the terms have completely different meanings in everyday usage. For example, face means the front part of a person's head from the forehead to the chin, or the corresponding part in an animal; in geometry a face is each of the surfaces of a solid, the faces of a cube. Mean in everyday use is miserly; in maths mean is the average of a set of numbers (i.e. add all of the numbers and divide by how many numbers there are). Another difficulty is the use of language in modern maths. It is no longer about being able to do calculations – one has to be able to understand the instructions.

Mathematical symbols representing ideas or processes are easier for a pupil on the spectrum to decipher.

However, the terms used for one concept are numerous. Let's take the idea of:
— minus, subtract, take away, what's the difference between, less than, left with, remainder, deduct, reduce, decrease. Can you think of any more?

So instead of 10 − 4 = 6
We have: What is 10 minus/subtract/deduct/take away/less than 4?
Or: What is the difference between 10 and 4?
Or: Reduce/decrease 10 by 4
The minus sign is also used as a negative, e.g. − 4° C.

We tend to take it for granted that these terms are interchangeable but, for the pupil with AS, these synonyms simply create confusion.

Another problem is that many pupils with AS will insist on using the first method they were taught to do a calculation. You will have to persuade the pupil that the new method is the best through logic – speed and efficiency – they'll get the sum done more quickly.

The problem with maths problems

Maths can be particularly problematical when answering problems with multiple parts to a question. One area of difficulty lies in the ability to process the information. The pupil has to be able to:

1 Scrutinize the problem
2 Find the relevant information
3 Analyse that information
4 Organize it in a logical sequence
5 Calculate the answer to the problem.

The whole process is quite challenging. One misstep and the whole sequence falls apart and you end up with an incorrect answer.

The pupil with AS will not be able to hold the answer to one part in their head as they proceed to the next step, due to a poor working memory. Therefore they need to be taught how to keep track of the answer as they do each part of the question.

This simple template is designed to help organize the answer, because examinations require that the sum is 'worked out' and all the steps put down on paper!

Template 11.1 – Break It Down

Parts of Question	Calculate	Answer – Carry Over
1.		
2.		
3.		
4.		
5.		
6.		
7.		

World knowledge

World knowledge is the knowledge gained through life experiences, through interaction with one's environment, objects, life events and other people. Research has shown that people with AS have problems processing world knowledge in context and making a judgement as to whether the knowledge is relevant in this context. They may ask: Why didn't they use cranes to build the pyramids?

Research suggested that the difference between NT and AS groups when handling world knowledge is probably related to difficulties that the AS group experienced remembering the exception rather than the rule. This is also evidence of a lack of flexible thinking. Be aware that when learning about a different place or time the pupil may have difficulties adjusting their perspective or thinking to accommodate the differences of an historical or geographical context and the attitudes of those who live in those places and times.

Be prepared for some idiosyncratic conclusions or inferences. Treat them seriously and explain the real differences. Laughing at these gaffs can be humiliating for the pupil.

Motivation

Motivating a child on the spectrum can be a bit of a challenge. They may be reluctant to do a task and will do everything they can to avoid it. The first question you need to ask is 'Does s/he feel s/he can do the task?' It may not be that they *won't* do it but that they *can't* do it. Also many pupils with AS will destroy work they do not feel is perfect. Using a laptop can help them produce a 'perfect' piece of work. They may not engage if you are using everyday subjects and objects. If you adapt to play to their strengths and interests you will encourage co-operation and make the task enjoyable for them.

In order to encourage the pupil to do the task, use their interest. Find out what television programme they enjoy watching. A pupil who is interested in Dr Who will be more motivated to add up using daleks or cybermen as counters; reading, grammar and spelling will be more purposeful if you use Dr Who stories; as will learning vocabulary when using words in sentences about Dr Who and the other characters.

Focus on teaching the *skill* and use resources that will engage them:

- Maths using daleks.
- Describe the Tardis.
- What does Dr Who do to solve this problem?
- Make up a world Dr Who might visit.
- What would Dr Who see if he went to Pompeii the day Mount Vesuvius erupted?
- What sort of person would be the ideal companion for Dr Who?
- If Dr Who had a healthy dinner, what food would he eat?
- Use a picture of Dr Who and label his clothes.

Reading texts and comprehension

Reading skills are important to all subjects. The member of staff who supports a pupil with AS will have to scrutinize the text and anticipate where there will be problems with communication – not just with ambiguity and figures of speech but with anaphoric cueing (shifting to the use of the pronoun in place of the noun), as well as historical settings, different places, other countries and cultures. Quite simply, they may actually understand very little of a fictional text.

A poor working memory can affect a pupil's ability to:

- Recall what they have just read;
- Follow instructions;
- Keep their place in the text;
- Sustain interest in the text or any task associated with it.

Supporting the pupil to understand reading texts

Research suggests that there are a number of strategies we can use to support comprehension:

- Provide clear titles to the text that inform the reader of the content.
- Prime the reader by reading a short summary of the content of the text – key words, ideas… draw the attention of the pupil to these key words and ensure they understand them.
- Read the text.
- Discuss the relationship of the text with the heading and the summary.
- If a task is to be done on the text, break it down into smaller bits related to the task and do one bit at a time.
- Use key words from the text in the questions.
- Ask the pupil to illustrate the passage as a way of showing comprehension. If there are fine motor skill problems, use Lego figures or clip art.

Some pupils with AS will have difficulty identifying and isolating the relevant text when doing a comprehension exercise and seeking the answers. Help them to identify key words by highlighting them from the question and doing a Word Hunt for key words in the text.

Use a Reading Blind to focus their attention on the section that they need to study.

Top Tip

Ask questions of your pupil to check that they have understood what they are reading. This is especially important if it is a literary text because they may struggle with characterization and context.

Reading blind

A Reading Blind is one or two pieces of blank, pastel-coloured paper used to cover the text the pupil is not reading. This helps them focus on the actual text being read.

A more sophisticated Reading Blind, for older pupils, is one that doubles up as a place to record notes on the text. See illustration below.

This can be used for any form of writing in any subject but is particularly useful when studying poetry, where an explanation of every figure of speech may need to be noted.

Materials

- 1 x A3 sheet of blank paper
- 2 x A4 sheets of paper lined or blank, as required
- Sellotape

Use Microsoft Publisher to position text and illustrations, then print onto A3 paper.

   Or:

- Print off or photocopy text onto A3 paper in two columns.
- Leave space around the perimeter for diagrams or illustrations, as required.
- Stick two pages of A4 sheets in between the two columns so they can be folded left or right and completely cover the text on either side.
- Fix illustration around perimeter of text.
- Cut the A4 pages into sections to hide some parts of the text but reveal others as necessary: paragraphs, verses, questions...
- The A4 page on the left covers/reveals the writing in the left column and the A4 page on the right covers/reveals the writing in the right column. See diagram below.
- Use the A4 pages to make notes on the revealed text.
- Photocopy notes onto single sheet for file.

JABBERWOCKY BY LEWIS CARROLL	Reading Blind
'Twas brillig, and the slithy toves Did gyre and gimble in the wabe; All mimsy were the borogoves, And the mome raths outgrabe.	Once fixed onto the A3 worksheet to cover all the text these sheets can be cut to hide sections of the text, as required, be it paragraphs or stanzas/lines of poetry.
'Beware the Jabberwock, my son! The jaws that bite, the claws that catch! Beware the Jubjub bird, and shun The frumious Bandersnatch!'	Two sheets of A4 are needed to cover each side of the paper because
He took his vorpal sword in hand: Long time the manxome foe he sought— So rested he by the Tumtum So rested he by the Tumtum tree,	• the other side of this sheet may be used to write notes relating to the text it covers;
And stood awhile in thought. And as in uffish thought he stood, The Jabberwock, with eyes of flame, Came whiffling through the tulgey wood,	• the text may be laid out differently on the other side.

Mind your language!

Use oral instruction sparingly: say exactly what you mean and mean exactly what you say.

Be positive in your instructions – tell them what to do rather than, 'Don't …'.

A pupil with autism will have difficulties understanding all aspects of language: spoken word, tone and intent, and may take everything you say literally. Idiomatic language is particularly problematic. As an exercise to assess the potential difficulties a pupil with AS might face, list the number of idioms and instances of ambiguous language that teachers and TAs use, unconsciously, while teaching.

A 'simple' instruction, commonly heard in the classroom, 'Write the title and the date in your books' may result in the pupil writing 'The title and the date' on the page, rather than 'Pharoahs of Egypt, 3rd January 2015'.

Top Tip

DIY instructions, which use as few words as possible, and lots of diagrams, are ideal for visual learners.

Difficulties with language

Poor receptive skills and auditory processing

The words they hear may run into each other and get all jumbled up; draw or write down instructions for pupils in a numbered list. Allow them to complete the first task before moving to the next one.

Pronoun reversal

Young children often make this mistake but the child with autism will persist in this error. Being addressed as 'you' in the family, the child may come to think that 'you' is one of their names. Use a comic conversation to illustrate correct pronoun usage and refer to other people as 'you' often, in their presence.

Anaphoric cueing

Check that the pupil understands what or to whom pronouns refer. Jack rides his bike to school every day. He is never late. Ask 'Who is he?' and point to 'He' in the sentence. Regular anaphoric cueing exercises will enable the pupil to recognize the way pronouns are used and develop greater comprehension of the text.

Hyperlexia

Be aware of the ability to read words far above what would be expected at the pupil's chronological age. They may read words perfectly but not understand them – check comprehension.

Reading homework may be of limited value for the hyperlexic pupil. They will do the reading but are unlikely to be able to tell you what they have read in any detail or relate to the characters. Film is more accessible and may be used to support a text.

They may use long words and pronounce words incorrectly in conversation. Compliment the pupil but give them the correct meaning. Other pupils will have a very advanced vocabulary and even words you may never have heard of, so 'check before correct'. My son used 'discombobulated' in an essay and his English teacher made the mistake of telling him there was no such word.

An excellent discussion explaining the difficulties pupils with ASCs experience and what can be done to support them can be found here: http://www.kansasasd.com/webinar_attach/1333040624_Web3_ReadingComp.pdf.

The Kansas Instructional Support Network, Reading Comprehension Strategies for Students with ASD: Skilled Readers – Webinar Feb 7, 2012, Trisha Self, PhD, CCC-SLP Wichita State University, Wichita, KS.

Visual disturbance and detail focus processing

Large passages of text may be distorted for the pupil or they may only be able to focus on a few words at a time.

If there is a problem, use Reading Blinds to block off the text that is not being read and write explanatory notes on the open blind as described above.

Literal interpretation

A lack of inhibition may also extend to work done in the classroom. The inability to suppress a literal translation of instructions, together with detailed focus processing, may lead to some very idiosyncratic responses to work set. Clear written instructions broken down to one task at a time, with visual cues if necessary, will be helpful to keep the pupil focused on the task. Speak literally.

Figurative language

Similes and metaphors will need to be translated and the connection or inference (see below) explained in detail because the pupil with AS will be unable to inhibit meaningless comparisons. A good example is taken from Gernsbacher and Robertson's (1999) research: Anna is like a swan. The intended analogy is that Anna is graceful and not that she has white feathers and flies.

Ask 'Why has "the writer" compared "this" with "that"?' And explain. They will not be able to work out the intention of the author or poet. Use illustrations to show similarities or differences and, in the case of differences, to move onto characteristics rather than visual appearance.

Idioms

When using idiomatic language, explain the meaning of the idiom. Play pairs card games matching common idioms to the meaning.

Homonyms

These are words that are spelt the same but have different meanings for example, fair (colouring), and fair (country festival), and fair (reasonable). They are also called **Homographs**.

Homophones

These are words that *sound* alike but are spelt differently and have different meanings: for example, bough (of a tree) and bow (bend forward in greeting).

The meaning of these types of words in context may be overlooked and very confusing, especially if words with the same spelling but with different meanings appear close together in a text. Check comprehension with a simple question about the word used in its context.

Inference

Inference is the conclusion arrived at based upon available evidence. The ability to infer is a complex skill utilizing short term memory if referring to something you have just read or done, for example an experiment in science; utilizing long term memory if referring back to a text read or work done in a previous lesson; and utilizing world knowledge if referring to information gained from experience. The skill is the ability to judge whether the inference is a reasonable one. In a pupil with AS the cognitive processing required to understand inference may be disordered. Allow time for processing.

In order to assess whether the pupil can 'infer', I use simple stories:

> Tim went fishing one morning. When he came home all his clothes were wet. What happened?

The correct answer is any logical reason for this: he fell in the river; it rained; a car drove through a puddle and splashed him; he rescued a dog that fell in the canal...

Or:

> Jack went off to ride his bike for the afternoon. As he turned on to the main road, there was a loud squeal of brakes and a thud. The ambulance arrived to take him to hospital twenty minutes later. Who was taken to hospital?

Questions to ask:
  'How do we know that...?'
  'Is there any information missing?'

A word of warning – your pupil may not be able to infer when anxious or distressed, whereas before they had no problems with inference.

Humour

Jokes may have to be explained. Most pupils with AS seem to love puns and slapstick humour, especially the classics such as Buster Keaton and Harold Lloyd, although they are likely to call it schadenfreude!

Irony, satire and sarcasm

These will have to be explained. Begin with the feeling of the person using these devices and what they hope to achieve.

Echolalia

This is repeating what has just been said as an answer. The pupil with AS may not have any other means of answering at the time other than to repeat what you have said. This may be a sign of stress if the pupil does not normally use this device to communicate; stuttering and mutism are also stress indicators. It may signal overload and shutdown.

Be aware that if you list choices and the pupil repeats the last item on that list, it might not be a selection based upon want or need but simply the repetition of the *last* word.

Pre-verbal communication skills

If used, these are likely to be done in the exaggerated manner you would find in a cartoon character or a much younger child. The pupil with AS will not be able to read another person's body language or work out a character's state of mind from the description of that character's body language in a text. You will have to explain these and practise decoding facial expressions and gestures, which are the clues to emotions.

Transfer of skills and lack of flexibility

Transfer of skills may be impaired due to a lack of flexibility. A skill, such as essay writing in English Language, that uses PEEL (Point Evidence Explanation Link) taught one day will not be automatically transferred to the next English lesson, in the same room but on another day. If this is particularly problematic it is sensible to have a booklet of how to take notes, write a report, sum up an experiment, and so on, that the pupil can refer to.

Grammar and spelling

Adherence to rules of grammar and spelling is often a strength. Try not to make any errors yourself: they may be pointed out to you in 'that' tone of voice! A pupil with AS is likely to draw attention to errors made because they think that you wouldn't want to make a mistake while teaching. Correct your error – they are invariably right – and thank them for noticing. They are not doing it to humiliate you.

Characterisation

Social blindness makes this a particular challenge. A pupil with AS will not be able to infer character from the person's actions or speech. Everything will have to be taught using Personality Plates.

Cognitive empathy or theory of mind: Placing oneself in another person's shoes

A pupil with autism may believe that you think exactly the same as they do. They are often confused if you tell them your opinion, which is completely different from theirs. Older children may change their answer to match yours, thinking they have made a social mistake. They need to be taught that differences of opinion are acceptable and their opinion is valid.

Imagination

Pupils with autism have wonderful imaginations – and are very creative people; think of the large number of inventors with Asperger Syndrome. What may be lacking is *flexibility*: they may want to do everything their own way or the way they were taught how to do it the first time. You will have to demonstrate good reasons for doing it a different way, like it being faster or the adult method.

Short sentences and literal language

When issuing instructions use short sentences and literal language. Word for word, convey meaning without ambiguity. Have visual supports if necessary.

Issuing commands/Rhetorical questions v Declarative language

Sometimes you may find that commands and rhetoric do not achieve the desired effect. For example 'Get up now!' or 'What do you think you're doing down there?'. A typical AS response might be 'No!' or 'Lying down!'. You could change your approach and make a suggestion as to what they could do instead of lying on the ground. 'Let's get you up and finish this, then we can go on the computer for 10 minutes.' Give them an activity they enjoy at the end of the task as a reward or incentive to complete the work.

If you have a pupil who finds text difficult to process quickly, use Communicate In Print 2 to create symbol-supported text (see below) for worksheets or letters home. With able pupils, use sparingly; every single word does not have to be illustrated.

Say exactly what you mean

Strategies for oral communication

- Avoid ambiguous language. Think before you speak!
- Use the least number of words you can.
- Do not use a nickname or tease them – they won't appreciate it and may get very upset, not understanding the intention or the emotion behind it.

- To focus the pupil's attention on you (not their eyes – don't insist they look at you) address them by their name first.
- In class the teacher usually writes the title of the day's lesson, the date and learning objectives on the board. Tell your pupil:

  '*John,* **copy** *what Mrs Smith has written on the whiteboard into your book.*'

  (It would be helpful if Mrs Smith wrote using a particular colour of ink for the text she wants copied into exercise books.)
- If your pupil has problems focusing on the board, copy a single piece of information such as 'Classwork', onto an A4 white board and tell your pupil to 'copy the writing on the board' into their book. Rub it off, then write the title, for example 'Ancient Egypt'. Rub that off, then write the date, for example '1st May, 2015'.
- Use the same words for the instruction in each lesson and the pupil will know what to expect and understand what you want him to do. Alternatively, have it written on a piece of paper using symbols, to which you draw their attention as and when necessary.
- Pencil an x lightly where you want them to write 'classwork', the 'title' and the 'date'.
- If the book is open on two pages and they start to write from the left, be aware that the line continues across to the end of the page on the right. Fold the exercise book over or place a blind (blank piece of paper) on the opposite page so that they only have the page they should write on available to them. Some pupils will be aware of this already.
- Relay verbal instructions one at a time. *Allow time for processing*; this may differ from pupil to pupil – be patient. Remember to use clear, unambiguous language; for example, do not say 'Paint the person sitting next to you', or you may find that pupil covered in paint!
- Do not repeat the instruction using different words. It will simply confuse them. Choose your words carefully from the outset and repeat the instruction exactly.
- Ask the pupil after the teacher has given an instruction:

  'What does Mrs Smith want you to do?'.

  Do not say, 'Do you understand?'.
- Written instructions are usually presented on a side of A4. This may be too much text. Use the Reading Blind, which is simply a blank piece of paper used to cover up the questions or steps they do not need to concentrate on.
- Do not assume that, after the instruction to open a book at a page, the pupil will automatically know to answer the questions on the page or read it. Ensure that no part of the instruction process is omitted. Explain each step to them. They will not know what to do unless you tell them.
- Ideally, there should be a school 'house style' regarding the way the page is titled and dated, but I've yet to see this in practice. There may be a subject style but each teacher will want it done his or her way. Why can't they all do it the same way? I don't know. Perhaps you could ask the question.
- If they make a mistake, tell them to put a single line through it. You may find the pupil will want to tear the page out and start again. This may happen at the end of a long piece of writing. Tell them that the 'rule' is to cross out the mistake by putting a neat line through it.
- Always assume they are doing their best. Do not rush the pupil when they are working at a task. They can't go any faster and if you interrupt them at the wrong moment, the house of cards they have so painstakingly built up may all come tumbling down and they will have to start from the beginning again.

Top Tip

Set up a discreet system by which they can tell you when they need help. Traffic signal: red – leave me alone: green – I need help!

Positive commentary v Confusing questions

Asking a child with autism a question may receive no response – they will feel pressurized and choose not to speak. Instead of asking them a question, describe what they are doing. When showing them how to do something, describe what you are doing as you are modelling it.

Set out the things they will need in front of you both, with a single set of visual instructions on a key fob open at the first instruction. Say, 'I take… (this piece) and put it (here)' … and wait for them to copy you. When they have done that, turn to the next illustration on the key fob and complete the next step, describing what you are doing, and wait for them to complete that before going on to the next.

Like paired reading, if they understand how you are doing the task and start to turn over the fob themselves and do the task on their own, then do the task silently unless they falter. This supports them to succeed independently.

Asking the right questions

When supporting a child with an ASC in a lesson never ask:

'How are you getting on?'

'Do you want my help?'

You will either get, 'Fine', or 'No.'

Very often a pupil with an ASC wants to do the task their way; they cannot tell whether they have difficulties or not; they don't want to draw attention to themselves; and they don't want to admit they don't understand.

Observe and ask 'What if you did this?'. Don't do the work for the pupil!

If strategies to support learning are used, it is likely the pupil will be able to access the curriculum with limited support. However, you should always check.

Some of the common pitfalls are: Can, Could, Would, Should, Will… are all verbs to avoid in questions because they invite a closed answer (see italics below).

Do not say:	Do say:
Can you tell me…? *Yes/No.*	Tell me…
Do you know …? *Yes/No.*	What do you know about…?
Is or was there a better solution to…? *Yes/No.*	What could he have done differently to effect a better outcome?

Why not write...? Why don't you ...?
They will tell you. Why not... because they
think you are asking them a question,
not making a suggestion.

Give clear instructions. Write...

What happened after...?
May only tell you the thing that happened
immediately after.

List the outcomes/results of...
Describe four different
after-effects of ...
What were the four effects ...

Find the meaning of...
May find the meaning but not write it
down or say it aloud.

and write it down

The following phrases are commonly found in examinations:

Illustrate your answer...
The pupil may think this means draw
the answer.

Give examples or
use evidence from the text...

What is the impact of...
What? There isn't one (collision).

Describe the effect of...

Comment on the writer's use of language...
It doesn't make sense because he is
silly.

Use a list or mnemonic as an aide memoire
for everything that should be included in a
comprehensive response to this type of
question.

Rather than asking an ambiguous question, it would be more effective and less confusing to instruct using the following words:

- Tell me... Write down... Show me... List... Explain... Describe... Plan... Use this method to... Design... Build... Compare... Contrast... Investigate... Analyze... Invent... Choose... Recommend...
- Be specific, by using quantity (a specific number) and focus attention on a theme.

Choices

- Choice is particularly difficult for an individual with AS. It may cause distress. Therefore, offer a choice between two things or none at all.
- When offering choices to a pupil with an ASC avoid giving a negative option at first. Offer two positive options based upon how much you think the pupil will be able to manage.
- Develop this skill with the family – ask them to offer choices and discuss the consequences.
- When the pupil understands that choices have consequences, offer a choice with negative consequences alongside a positive choice to help them make the right decision.

Top Tip

Teach the pupil to identify and decode key words in order to produce an appropriate response.

12 Handwriting difficulties, poor working memory and scribing for a pupil with AS

You may find yourself scribing for a pupil on the autism spectrum. Handwriting is a complex skill we take for granted. The pupil with AS may find it difficult for a number of reasons. Proprioception difficulties and poor fine motor skills may make handwriting awkward due to problems in exerting the correct amount of pressure for the task and forming the letters. Hypermobility and poor muscle tone are also associated with ASCs and they may be unable to hold writing or drawing tools properly. They may also experience pain while attempting to do this.

The working memory is the process by which our brains store information while doing a task. The information is put on standby until needed. A poor working memory means that the information is forgotten, sometimes immediately after the instruction is given. This is very common when the instructions are oral, as typically experienced in classrooms. If the pupil has a poor working memory and difficulties with organizing their thoughts and ideas (planning) and physically writing, the cognitive processing needed to do all these tasks simultaneously makes the whole process very slow, but you will have to be quick to take down what your pupil has said because they will be unlikely to remember and repeat it.

While you are supporting your pupil in class by taking notes, or doing any written work for them, have them dictate the work to you. They will be quite happy to sit back and let you do the work, taking notes directly from the teacher, but in order to engage them in the lesson you will have to ask them to direct you in your note-taking and doing the task set. You can explain that, when they sit their examinations, the scribe will not be able to write down anything unless dictated by the candidate.

Pupils with AS will need to be taught how to dictate and you need to practise taking dictation with the pupil beforehand. Because their poor working memory means that they may be unable to repeat a sentence they have literally just spoken, it therefore becomes even more important that they learn to work with a scribe at a rate where the scribe can write efficiently and accurately. Also don't forget to practise drawing diagrams and graphs. Describing these can be very tricky. They may choose to draw these themselves.

Scribing in examinations

Check the rules of the examination: SATs in Years 2 and 6 and the 11+. Your pupil will be relying on you to do a good job for them when scribing in examinations and needs to be able to trust that you will. The pupil will also be nervous, although they may not appear so, and establishing a rapport with them will enable you to reassure them appropriately.

A scribe needs to be able to:

• Concentrate for a long period of time.

- Remember accurately what the pupil has dictated without having to ask them to repeat themselves.
- Write at speed for a long period of time: practise.
- Write legibly – the pupil should be able to read your writing as well as the examiner.
- Write accurately.

How to scribe for a pupil with AS

- Arrive in good time to reassure the candidate that you are ready and happy to work for them.
- Explain to the candidate what you can do as their scribe.
- Explain to the candidate what you cannot do as their scribe.
- Be patient. Be quiet. Be still.
- It may take the candidate with AS some considerable time to read through the question booklet and choose which question they want to answer.
- Be prepared. Be patient. Be quiet. Be still.
- It may take the candidate with AS time to organize their thoughts and begin dictating.
- When they begin to dictate, write down their words as quickly as possible.
- Let them know when you have finished writing by making an encouraging noise or prearranged signal for them to continue dictating.
- Ensure they can see what you have written.
- At the end of the examination congratulate them on a job well done.

Pupils who are likely to need scribes during an examination should be taught how to dictate to a scribe properly as soon as possible because it is a completely different set of skills.

How to dictate to a scribe

Position

- The pupil should sit close enough to the scribe to be able to see what you are writing.
- Have the pupil sit on the same side of the hand you write with. If you are right-handed, have the pupil sit on your right hand side; left-handed, have them sit to your left.
- Check they can read what you are writing.
- Make sure that they are not in the way of your writing.

Speaking to the scribe

Teach the pupil to:

- Speak clearly.
- Establish a good dictation speed that you are both comfortable with.
- Ensure the pupil has a bottle of water: they will get thirsty.

Teach them to organize themselves before answering the question

- Read the question three times.
- Analyze the question – what do they have to do?
- Break the question down into sections using subheadings from the key words in the question.
- Think about what they want to say.
- Dictate a short plan, a list of key words or notes to remind them what they want to include in their answer/essay.
- Look at the plan regularly.
- Delete each point off the plan after it has been included in the essay.

Teach them how to dictate

- Use short sentences.
- Ask you to read aloud what they have dictated to help them think about what they want to say next.
- Need to change anything? They need to ask you, the scribe, to delete the word, phrase, sentence or paragraph or move it.
- Continue dictating.
- They should take time to think about what they want to say.
- Checking the time.
- Diagrams and graphs – the scribe must be told exactly how to draw these. Give one instruction at a time.
- Check their work before the end of the examination.
- Tell the scribe what they want corrected.

When it's all over, don't forget to praise your pupil for a job well done. And give yourself a pat on the back too. It's very stressful for both of you.

All these skills will become more important in a secondary school, where they will have to learn to dictate to a scribe for high stakes examinations. Learning good dictation skills as early as possible will enable them to do this efficiently and reduce anxiety levels later on.

13 Written assignments

Be specific

The pupil with AS needs to know exactly what is expected of them. State how many words, sentences, paragraphs or pages they are expected to write (depending on the size of the pupil's handwriting if the last two are employed).

Strategies used in KS 1

Writing frames and colour coding to support written work will be of benefit to the pupil right up to Year 6 and beyond. Structure and uniformity help pupils with AS feel secure and competent. Use the templates provided here to support the older pupil. They will provide transition into secondary practices.

High stakes examination assessments

Tell them to aim to write the *maximum* number of words, not the minimum! In my experience, when a teacher tells a class the assignment should be 100–200 words, the AS pupil will stop writing as near to 100 words as they can. They may even stop at 100 words dead, without considering whether they have finished the sentence or not! There may be no shape to the essay. It will simply finish at the word count without development or conclusion.

Or they may continue until they feel that they have finished, with no regard for the time and the fact that they have to answer several parts of one question.

Planning

The pupil with AS will be very reluctant to plan their work. It will be of value to give credit for writing a plan. This will encourage them to write one and they need to do this to keep track of the task they are doing. If the plan is part of the required process from the outset, then they are likely to plan their work, to their advantage, throughout.

Demonstrate the advantages of planning using the appropriate templates.

Worksheets and written instructions

Worksheets are often written in close type with lots of instructions. These are often overwhelming for a pupil with AS. A more effective form of presentation is to break it down to one instruction per page in A5 format.

The Task Instructions template is designed for older pupils, to clarify the process in the absence of someone to prompt them, and it is, therefore, an ideal tool for breaking down homework assignments. The initial instruction includes the number of questions or tasks they have to complete overall. At the end of each page is a prompt to proceed from one part of the task to the next.

The sheets are designed to be photocopied back to back, to form an A5 booklet with the centre sheet photocopied as often as needed, depending on the length of the task. Although the sheet is designed to be flexible, I recommend you only write one task per page. The booklet can then be folded over so that the pupil only has to focus on one task at a time.

Don't forget to write down the number of the page if you use the extra sheets.

Template 13.1 – Task Instructions

Name: ....

Subject: ....Class: ....

Teacher: ....

Title: ....

....

....

....

....

....

Date set: ....

Turn over page.

The end.

Well done.

You have now completed your task.

Hand it in to: ....

Room: ....

By: ....

Complete: ....

Number of words @ ....

No less than .... words.

No more than .... words.

Remember to: ....

Go to page

2

Go to page

Go to page

Writing templates for English Language, History, Geography and Religious Education

Due to Executive Function Deficit, which is an inability to plan or organize oneself effectively, a pupil with AS may have trouble starting a piece of writing, sustaining a piece of writing, and ending it! The younger pupil will benefit from planning their story using illustrated prompts. Most pupils with AS will be reluctant to *plan* but, if ever a pupil needed to do this, it is definitely the individual with AS.

The Writing Templates cover a range of subjects:

- Writing a Story – for younger pupils
- Creative Writing
- Lego for younger pupil
- Factual Essay Plan using PEEL (Point Evidence Explanation Link)
- Inference
- Fact or Opinion
- Compare and Contrast
- GAPS – Genre, Audience, Purpose and Style
- Writing to Argue, Inform, Persuade or Advise + Links

Encourage the pupil to tick off the points made after they have written them, which enables them to see their progress while developing a sustained piece of writing.

.... writes a story

About...
....

....
....

....
....

....
....

Creative writing

Focus the pupil's attention on what is required using the creative writing template. This is based on the development of a story, not the number of paragraphs.

Use the boxes to outline the story:

- Set the scene.   WHERE?
- Introduce the characters.   WHO?
- Create the problem or challenge.   WHAT AND WHY?
- *Include dialogue.*   *WHO SAYS WHAT TO WHOM?*
- Describe the struggle.   HOW?
- The climax.   SUCCESS or FAILURE

This is very loosely based on the beginning, middle and end format but with more guidance for development of character.

Drawing stick figures in the first column to emphasize the story scenario reinforces the idea and provides an illustration of the progression of a story.

Develop their skills by focusing on one step at a time:

- Set the **scene**.   Descriptive detail reflecting the mood
- Introduce the **characters**.   Describe 1 or 2 of the people
- *Include dialogue.*   Conversation or argument (avoid 'said')
- What is the **conflict?**   Why? Action (avoid 'went')
- How? Describe the **struggle**.   Descriptive detail – action
- The Climax   Resolution – action, reflection

Top Tip

Find out what sort of story the pupils are going to be asked to write about and have a selection of pictures to illustrate the scene, characters and some of the action for the pupil to refer to.

For example, a ghost story may have a couple of figures walking in a wood at night, and an adventure story may involve people stranded on some rocks as the tide comes in. Use the pupil's interest as a starting point, if appropriate. A science fiction fan may be interested in writing a story set in space, fantasy in another world or journeys on the Orient Express. Do not give more than two choices.

Template 13.3 – Creative Writing

Title:..

....

Where? Scene	
Who? Characters	
What happens? How? Why? The Plot The Conflict	
The CLIMAX! The END	

Using Lego

Often a favourite toy for a child with an ASC, Lego can be used as a motivational tool across the subjects. Lego mini-figures cover a vast number of characters and scenarios that often form part of an autistic child's interests: princesses, knights, ghosts, cowboys, space men and characters from famous books and films; aliens, elves, dwarves and mermaids; together with animals, dinosaurs, vehicles and plants. Create a visual scene based upon the pupil's interest to give them a starting point from which to begin their story. If you can, collect enough figures and pieces to make three scenarios of one story – you can build up a visual scene to support learning in a variety of subjects. Lego have a Story Starter set for this very purpose, which is supported by an App.

At first, the pupil is likely to recount a story from the films, but if you add another figure, perhaps representing the child, and add them to the scene, the story can then be written in the first person 'I', or used to recount an event in the pupil's life. Move on to characters representing non-specific people and ask the child to enact a scene related to a specific idea: the runaway dog, or the cat stuck up a tree.

Story building

1 Set the Scene
   Give the child an assortment of bricks selected to support the topic of the lesson and use that as a starting point. Build the set.
2 Introduce the character/s
   Select mini-figures
   Or start with a figure and ask the child to build a scene based on the figure. For example, spaceman – the child may build the control room of a space ship or the surface of a planet.
3 Give them a problem – an alien appears, the space ship is broken…
4 If you only have one set of Lego, then take a photograph, print it off and move on to the next scene.
5 Once the story has been photographed, then it can be written up with reference to the Lego sets.
6 Draw attention to details inserted in the sets to create atmosphere – flowers in a vase or a cat by the door.

Comic strip or graphic story

- Photographing and printing off scenes can also be used to create a graphic story or comic strip. Insert speech bubbles to help build dialogue.
- A comic strip, built up in this way, can also be used to explore social situations and develop useful skills for appropriate interaction.

Film using Stop Motion

- Plan a very short story in a single setting.

- Collect all the materials you need, for example, a green towel for an outdoor scene in a field, blue backdrop – pillow case, coloured paper or a painted background; BluTack to fix the figures.
- Props – e.g. build a house, market, ship or a farm and collect figures.
- Set up the scene for the beginning of the story.
- Light it with a lamp or a torch.
- Set up the camera in a fixed position. Focus it on the 'scene'.
- Take a photograph.
- Move the figures in sequences by moving body parts to create the story, taking photographs of each scene. Note – you will need lots of pictures to make even a short film.
- Once the story is finished, upload the photos to the computer.
- Use Windows Movie Maker or iMovie software to make the film.
- Create title page and credits in PowerPoint and add to the beginning and end of the film.
- Set each camera shot to run for a short duration so that they flow quickly from one to another creating an animation.
- Add the soundtrack.
- Play!

There are a number of websites which will help you with the film-making program you have. A good one, showing you how to use both Windows Movie Maker or iMovie, is http://www. wikihow.com/Create-a-Stop-Motion-Animation.

Lego can be used for a variety of subjects:

- **English** – all figures and brick sets – let your imagination loose.
  - Factual writing can be done using animals, space ships, other vehicles or even city structures and services – civil and emergency.
- **Maths** – use Lego Maths set.
- **Science** – explore science by replicating experiments with Lego bricks or telling the story of great scientific figures and their discoveries.
- **History** – there are Fairytale and Historic Minifigure sets, which have castles, kings, queens and knights. Adapt Minifigures by painting Roman clothing on the chest.
- **Geography** - see Viola the Volcano Pops on the website below, based upon the true story of Parícutin, Mexico.
  - A trip to Legoland with its world landmarks is a good way to support work done on a topic in school.
- **RE** – Brendan Powell Smith created the Brick Testament with great attention to detail for all the Bible stories from the Old and New Testaments.
- **Technology** – Lego Mindstorm for older pupils – building robots.
- **Art** – projects based around Lego bricks could be very rewarding for the pupil.

Lego collage: the variety of pieces makes it a very flexible medium. Google 'Lego collage' and you will come up with numerous pictures from great masters to portraits of superheroes!

Street Art: place mini-figures in the school environment to turn a crumbling brick wall into a cliff or a puddle into a lake and take photos. Lego has become a popular medium for sculpture; see the work of Nathan Sawaya, who had an exhibition in London in 2014; and Sean Kenney. Look at their work online.

Websites

Lego Story Starter Pack https://education.lego.com/en-gb/preschool-and-school/upper-primary/7plus-storystarter/curriculum-pack

Lego Story Starter App https://education.lego.com/en-gb/preschool-and-school/lower-primary/6plus-storystarter/storyvisualizer

Lego Maths https://education.lego.com/en-gb/preschool-and-school/lower-primary/6plus-moretomath/introducing-moretomath

http://www.thebricktestament.com/home.html

http://www.wikihow.com/Create-a-Stop-Motion-Animation

Brick artists

http://brickartist.com/category/gallery/ for Nathan Sawaya's work.

http://www.seankenney.com

Template 13.4

1. Using Lego to 'Build' a Story		
	Illustrations	Photographs
	Prompt	Pupil's work
Where and When?		
Who? Characters		
What? Problem		
How? Events		
Ending		

2. Using Lego to Illustrate a Particular Event		
Subject:	Illustrations	Photographs
	Prompt	Pupil's work
Where and When?		
Who?		
What?		
Result		

3. Lego Storyboard or Instructions

Using Lego to Create		
Subject: Art	Illustrations	Photographs
Original Artwork	Lego Version	Pupil's work
Landscape		
Portrait		
Abstract		
Sculpture		

Factual essay writing

By including the levels attained for completing each part, the pupil with AS will see what he will gain (literally) from writing in this style. Write the levels at Key Stage 3 in the headline of the template thus:

POINT Level 3	EVIDENCE Level 4/5	EXPLAIN Level 5/6	LINK Level 7

It can be used to prepare for essays in most subjects about any topic.

- Teach the pupil to read the question carefully and decode language.
- They should be encouraged to identify and highlight the key words, which tell them what they have to do.
- Check they have understood the question by asking the following questions:

What is the title telling you to do?

How are you going to do this?

What do you think of the…?

- Pay particular attention to the opening/introductory paragraph of the essay. I recommend the pupil extract words from the title to discuss in general terms.
- Pupils with AS, having difficulty placing themselves into another person's shoes, may be under the impression that you and everyone else thinks the same as they do. Validate their opinion, providing they can back it up with good reasons.

Template 13.5 – Factual Essay

Title/Question:...

....

POINT	EVIDENCE	EXPLAIN	LINK

Timeline

The 'Timeline' is a simple but very effective tool, which pupils can easily draw for themselves and brings order to the task.

Its potential uses are to plot:

- Dates
- Development Tracker, e.g. volcanic eruption, plant growth, events leading to...
- Time Management – cooking
- Any plan which requires the pupil to be aware of 'time'.

To make a timeline, take a rule and draw a line down the left hand side of the page or across the bottom of the page; for example, this 2 hour timeline for a cookery lesson with 10, 30, and 60 minute 'lines'.

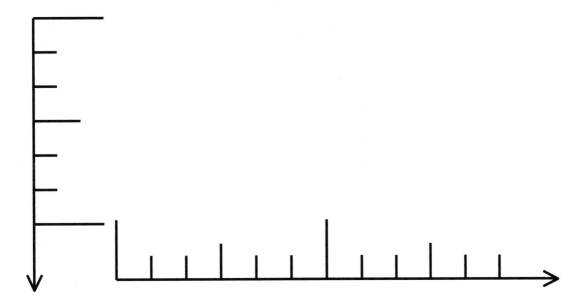

Maps

Maps are useful tools when working with an AS pupil because place in the context of the lesson may have little meaning for them. It would also be useful to have north to south or east to west noted with a scale of distance. Remember that abstract concepts may be difficult ideas to grasp for a pupil with an ASC.

Carry a folder of maps. I had copies of the British Isles, World, Europe, Asia, Australia and New Zealand, North America and South America. You never know when you might need them and not just for the lesson. I have also used them to play guess the country or capital city to distract a pupil.

Website

http://www.freeusandworldmaps.com/html/WorldRegions/WorldRegionsPrint.html

Inference

Inference may be confusing to a pupil with AS. They are being asked to look at the evidence and refer to their world knowledge, make a connection between the two and come to a conclusion based upon the information given. The evidence to support the conclusion is in the form of a clue in the text rather than an actual statement. The pupil needs to be taught how to read 'between the lines'.

John left the house carrying his bucket and spade.
Where is he going? To the beach.
How do you know this? What is the clue to the inference he is going to the beach?
He is carrying his bucket and spade.

John left the house carrying his bucket and spade.

Top Tip

Use the magnifying glass symbol to alert the pupil that when reading this passage and answering questions on it, they have to search for clues and make inferences from the text.

If you ask the question: 'What do you infer from this passage?' the most likely response will be a repeat of the action described.

Differentiated inference templates

1   Copy the TEXT being analysed into the Inference Template in the column: 'I read this'.
2   Write down the FACTS in the second column: 'I know that'.
3   Write down the CLUES in the third column: 'The clue is…'.
4   Write down the INFERENCE in the fourth column: 'I conclude that…'.

Use Inference Template 2 when you want to develop the skill of reading the text and predicting what is going to happen next.

Start teaching inference by giving the answers and asking the pupil to find the inferred evidence to support this. Use different colours relating to the questions being asked, e.g. a) circle clues in blue, b) green, c) red…

Inference exercise

1   Read the following passage.
2   Put a circle round the clues.

"John, go down to the shop and buy a bottle of milk, please," his mother asked as she handed him her purse.

John went into the hall and pulled on his coat and woolly hat. He sat on the stairs to pull on his wellies. Then out he went, slamming the door behind him. She watched his hunched figure stomping off down the road.

Fifteen minutes later he returned, marched straight into the kitchen and put the milk down on the table with a thump, glowering at her as he returned to the hall.

3   Where are the clues that tell you:
   a)   John and his mother have run out of milk.
   b)   It is cold outside.
   c)   It is wet outside.
   d)   John doesn't want to go.
   e)   John feels cross.
   f)   John is angry with his mother.

You should get something like this. However, don't be surprised if the pupil doesn't realize that 'she' refers to John's mother and 'he' to John. Some pupils have difficulties with anaphoric cueing.

"John, *go down to the shop and buy a bottle of milk*, please," his mother asked as she handed him her purse.

John went into the hall and *pulled on his coat and woolly hat*. He sat on the stairs to *pull on his wellies*. Then out he went, *slamming the door* behind him. She watched *his hunched figure stomping off* down the road.

Fifteen minutes later he returned, *marched straight into the kitchen and put the milk down on the table with a thump, glowering at her* as he returned to the hall.

Template 13.6 – Inference 1

I read the text below:	I know these FACTS: ✓	The CLUE is:	I conclude the INFERENCE is:

Inference 2 – I Predict

I read:	I know these FACTS ✓	The CLUE **S** are	I predict that this will happen:

Inference 3

TEXT	FACTS ✓	CLUE 🔍 S	INFERENCE

Fact or Opinion?

Differentiating between fact and opinion can be challenging for any pupil. Facts can be described as what can be proved to be true and Opinion is what someone feels or believes about something. Use the magnifying glass symbol for facts and the thought bubble for opinion.

On a sheet of paper draw a large magnifying glass and a thought bubble. Have a number of facts and opinions written on strips of paper, and get the pupil to sort them by putting the facts on the magnifying glass and opinions on the thought bubble; for example, a lion: lives in Africa, king of the animals, likes sunbathing, male lions have a mane, baby lions are called cubs…

A harder task will be to select and differentiate between fact and opinion in a passage of text. Photocopy the Fact or Opinion? Template onto A3 size paper and insert the text you wish to analyze in the middle. Using different coloured pens, underline the facts in one colour and opinions in another and ask the pupil to explain the reasons why they think they are facts or opinions in the appropriate column on either side of the text.

Template 13.7 – Fact or Opinion?

FACT	TEXT	OPINION

Different Points of View – Compare and Contrast

The following four Writing Templates may be used to prepare for writing about two different things or points of view. The Callouts are for Speech, and Thought Bubbles for thoughts or opinions.

- Two points of view (opinions)
- Compare and contrast
- Speech bubbles
- Boxes and bubbles

The Conversations Templates are designed to be flexible in order to support a number of tasks.

Two Points of View using thought bubbles can be used for opinions about a topic and in social skills lessons to demonstrate that individual people have different thoughts about a particular event.

Compare and Contrast The template is designed to show a clear separation of ideas to help organize their thinking and make the writing process easier. It may be used for any topic in any subject where the pupil has to consider two objects, ideas, characters, historical periods, countries. Animal or vegetable? Hot or cold lunches? Christian or Hindu? I think this and you think that? Anything!

The Speech Callouts can also be used to develop the writing of dialogue in an English essay or an argument.

This template may also be used to conduct a basic Comic Conversation – questions and answer.

The Boxes and Callout template (page 176) can be used in a variety of different ways:

- Figurative language – analyzing simile and metaphor.
- Similarities and differences when looking at a topic – using the boxes in between the speech callouts for agreement (comparison) and the speech callouts for disagreement (contrast).
- Giving two answers to one question.
- Good points and bad points when making a decision.
- The right thing to do and the wrong thing to do.

The templates are designed to be flexible and meet a variety of scenarios in school.
The last template is for the older pupil to develop an argument in an essay.

Top Tip

Different writing styles are used in different subjects, and an awareness of the appropriate style of writing for each subject will benefit the pupil.

Template 13.8 – 2 Points of View

I think this...   S/he thinks that...

Compare and/or Contrast

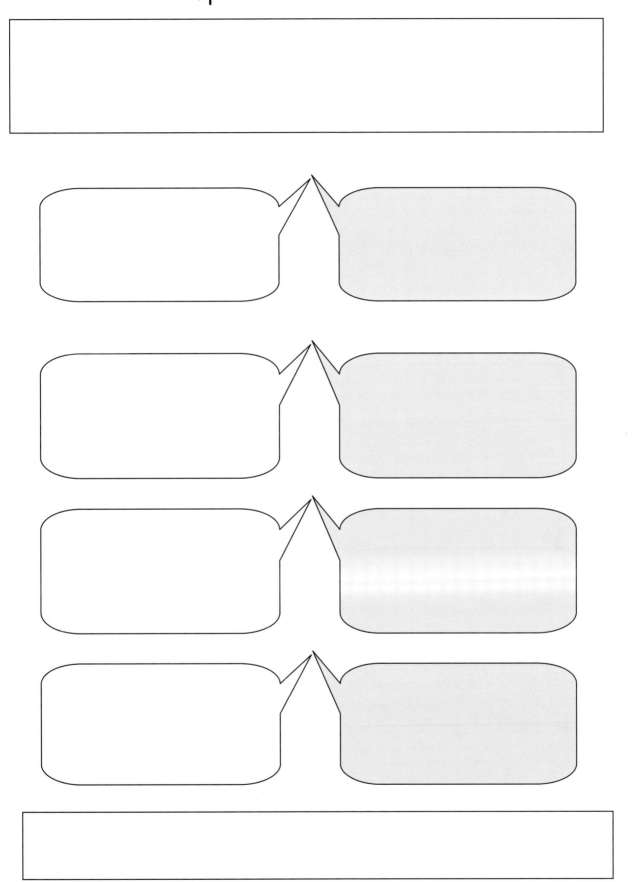

Writing to Argue, Inform, Persuade and Advise (KS2)

You cannot assume that the pupil with AS will infer from the information given who the audience is or the correct style of writing they should adopt.

The first template is used to focus the pupil's attention on this decision. The simple mnemonic GAPS is to remind them what they should take into consideration:

- **G**enre (type of writing e.g. story, report, analysis);
- **A**udience (who are you writing for?);
- **P**urpose (why are you writing this?);
- **S**tyle (what style or form should it take to serve the purpose and appeal to the intended audience?).

This can be used in any subject.

And the last template is to help them construct an essay using link phrases for a fluent writing style.

Template 13.9 – GAPS: Genre, Audience, Purpose and Style

Essay Title:		
Key Words:		
Genre – I will write a: letter, newspaper article, speech, information leaflet, advertisement	because:	
Audience – the people who are going to read this are:		
Purpose – I am writing this to:		
Style – therefore, I will write in a friendly/formal/humorous...		Style:
Writing devices I will use are (rhetorical question, repetition – power of three, personal experience, statistics, facts, opinion, plea):		
Vocabulary – words I shall use:		

Template 13.10 – Argument Writing: 2 Points of View

INTRODUCTION The question of.../ the idea that is....

This may be true but

It is often said ...

This argument does not convince me...

Nevertheless,

It has been suggested...

I am convinced that...

However,

Opponents of ... say that...

I disagree with this because...

Alternatively,

Advocates of this... say...

In spite of that, I ...

To sum up... Finally... Therefore, I would argue that...

14   English Literature

Literature is difficult for pupils with AS because of their lack of social awareness and inability to place themselves in another person's shoes. As visual learners, some have excellent memories for dialogue from films they have seen. Observe your target pupil and try to identify how they learn best. It may be more effective for them to have illustrated texts.

- Use graphic novels and plays rather than plain text. There are a wide range of graphic novels: Tintin, Asterix, Alex Rider series and old classics such as Tom Sawyer, Call of the Wild and Sherlock Holmes, available for older readers. John McDonald's Shakespeare plays are differentiated to 3 levels – original text, plain English and shortened versions. They are also supported with interactive motion comics, using celebrated Shakespearean actors, available to buy at: www.classicalcomics.com.
- Watch the film of the play or novel. An authentic portrayal of the play in its proper context is best.
- Use visual references relating to the text. You can illustrate a text by drawing a scene, using stick figures. These may be made easily recognizable as the characters through the use of simple, visual references, symbols and colours, which represent physical characteristics or personality traits. No need to draw faces.

   This type of illustration is devised to support the understanding of relationships and dialogue and therefore uses speech bubbles. The pupil identifies the appropriate quotations from the text and transcribes them onto the cartoon.
- Another format to support teaching poetry is to divide A3 paper into 6 sections for illustrations with a space beneath the picture for 1 to 2 lines of a poem. Another space for notes or a reference to the relevant text may also be incorporated into the design.

   The pupil should copy out the lines of poetry beneath the relevant illustration.
- Films – when watching films, be aware that the dramatic licence may be accepted as a true representation of the text.

Top Tip

Use original text audio books or recordings because some individuals with AS have an excellent memory for film dialogue and/or audio recordings.

Personality Plates

'Plate' 1 has a single 'face'.

Draw the character on the oval shape using symbolic features: a caricature. Draw visual references next to the personality profile. List aspects of the character's personality with a suitable quotation under evidence, and page references.

The drawings do not have to be great, just enough to get ideas across.

The template is designed to draw attention to the need to note a number of personality facts and textual evidence for them. Too often the AS pupil will give a single reason in response to a question because that is all he has been asked for. Teach the pupil to give as many different reasons as they can think of.

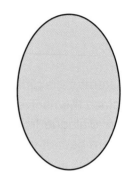

There are two **Character Templates**. Comparing Characters has two 'heads' but can also be used for discussing historical characters, or morphed into animals. Items can be drawn or stuck into the middle of the oval. They are designed to be flexible.

The two-headed template is also a good tool to use when teaching Social Skills or Cognitive Empathy exercises to enable the pupil to see that while he thinks about one thing based upon what happened. Another person may have a completely different viewpoint.

Template 14.1

Character's name:...

Personality Fact	Evidence

is...

because...

....

....

....

....

....

....

....

....

....

....

....

....

....

....

....

....

....

....

....

Template 14.2 – Comparing Characters

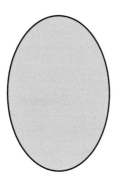
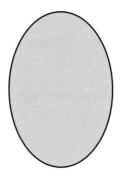

Name...

Fact...

Evidence...

....

F..

Ev..

....

F..

Ev..

....

F..

Ev..

....

F..

Ev..

Name...

....F

....Ev

....

....F

....Ev

....

....F

....Ev

....

....F

....Ev

....

....F

....Ev

Poetry

Understanding poetry is difficult for the pupil with AS. It is a highly sophisticated use of language both in the grammatical and creative sense. Humorous poetry can pose problems; nonsense verse may be rejected as silly and meaningless or embraced and mimicked in everyday speech for days. Individuals with autism also enjoy puns and making up their own 'jokes'! Encourage this exploration of language. You may discover that the pupil has a very interesting way of expressing themselves in their own poetry.

Original metaphors and similes will cause major problems. Explain each in detail, as discussed in Language Difficulties. Narrative poems with few figures of speech are easier to understand.

Illustrate the poem

- Create a booklet of challenging poetry. Place the poem and notes on the left hand side of the booklet with the illustrations on the right. The pupil can then link the illustration to the relevant line in the poem. If this is laminated, dry wipe pens can be used and the resource reused.
- Visual references establish the context, be it historical, geographical or social. A glossary of relevant and dictionary terms can also be incorporated as notes on each page for immediate reference to support learning and understanding. It is a lot of work initially but, once done, is available to generations of pupils.
- Create a work mat on A3 paper with the poem in 1 or 2 columns in the centre of the sheet, surrounded by images relating to the content. Fix a reading blind in the centre.
- Make PowerPoint handouts, illustrated with relevant images, 2 lines of poetry per slide, 3 slides to a page, with lines for jotting down notes. Cut up the poem into two lines. Jumble them for the pupil to match the right couplets to each slide.
- Colour coding the text to highlight imagery – metaphor, simile and symbol, characterization, theme, or any aspect of the text you want to focus on – may also be helpful. Always use the same colour to illustrate the type of text you want to reinforce. Using blue for metaphor in one poem and then red to highlight metaphor in another poem is not helpful – be consistent.
- Background notes on the writer's inspiration, historical context and the literary form of the text may be added to provide world knowledge cueing for the pupil before reading the text.
- Add no more information than is necessary to support understanding of the text.
- Filming a poem either in an animated version using Lego, or acting out the poem, helps comprehension.

Top Tip

Differentiate poems using clip art for nonsense and humorous verse and photographs or line drawings for descriptive or serious narrative poetry.

Poetry analysis – Step by step (KS2)

It is more helpful to the pupil with AS to label things, using their correct terms, right from the start. The mnemonic is a useful device when supporting the inclusion of a number of elements in a complex task for someone with a poor working memory. CATS DIRRT FO is for KS2 pupils to write a comprehensive response to the unseen poem. The notes in the margin are for your guidance to support the pupil.

1 **Content** – what the poem is about.
2 **Aim** – what the poet wants to say.
3 **Theme** – the big idea/subject of the poem, a feeling.
4 **Syntax** – the positioning of the words in a sentence and their relationship to each other.
5 **Diction** – the poet's choice or use of words to express meaning.
6 **Imagery** – figures of speech that produce a special effect, making you see pictures in your mind.
    – **Illustrated Imagery** – use boxes for pictures of the poet's images. The first box should contain a literal interpretation of the image, for example, 'she was as graceful as a swan' should have a picture of a swan in the 'picture' box and in the 'meaning' box a picture of a graceful woman. You will have to explain the connection.
7 **Rhythm** – a regular arrangement of sounds, and of stressed and unstressed syllables, giving a sense or feeling of movement; metre is the arrangement of words and syllables, or feet, in a rhythmic pattern according to their length and stress; a particular pattern or scheme, for example, Iambic pentameter = ' / or di dah (short long) x 5 -/-/-/-/-/.
8 **Rhyme** – a pattern of words that have the same final sounds at the ends of lines in a poem. A Rhyme Scheme is plotted using a letter of the alphabet to identify each rhyme sound. Begin with the letter a, then b, and so on. See the rhyme scheme for the first stanza of *Charge of the Light Brigade* by Alfred, Lord Tennyson below. Underlining the lines in different colours corresponding to the letter will help you see whether or not there is a pattern in the rhyme:

Half a league, half a league,	a
Half a league onward,	b
All in the valley of Death	c
Rode the six hundred.	b
'Forward, the Light Brigade!	d
Charge for the guns' he said:	d
Into the valley of Death	c
Rode the six hundred.	b

9 **Tone** – a quality or character of the voice expressing a particular feeling or mood.
10 **Form** – structure and organization in a piece of writing, the outward appearance, if appropriate: a calligram is a poem formatted in the shape of a picture. Certain types of poems have a specific number of lines, for example, limerick – 5, sonnet – 14.
11 **Opinion** – Write what you think of the poem and explain why.

This may also be the basis for an 11-paragraph essay, one step at a time, using the notes made in Template 14.3.

Template 14.3

POEM TITLE: .... POET ....

TYPE of POEM: ....

TASK	EXAMPLE	QUOTATIONS	COMMENTS
Content A summary – What is the poem about?			
Allusion – reference to other literature?			
Aim – poet's intention. Why is the poet writing about this?			
Good story, interesting character, sharing an experience....			

TASK	EXAMPLE	QUOTATIONS	COMMENTS
Theme: what is the main idea? Love, jealousy, time passing, nature, religion, death.			
Syntax: the order of the words in the lines. Fluent sentences, clumsy grammar. Slang or Dialect. Voice – a way of speech peculiar to the persona (a monologue) or the poet's 'voice'?			

TASK	EXAMPLE	QUOTATIONS	COMMENTS
Diction: alliteration – repetition of consonant sounds;			
assonance – repetition of vowel sounds;			
onomatopoeia – word sounds like the sound it describes;			
sibilance – sss;			
caesura – pause mid line;			
enjambment – idea goes from one line/stanza to another without pause.			

TASK	EXAMPLE	QUOTATIONS	COMMENTS
Imagery: Simile (cue like/as).			
Metaphor:			
Personification – inanimate object given human characteristics – the wind screamed in fury. Pathetic fallacy: human feelings given to nature – smiling sun, cruel wind.			

TASK	PICTURE		QUOTATIONS	COMMENTS
	Image	Meaning		
Insert or draw a picture of the image into the EXAMPLE box.				
(Imagery includes the following:				
Simile, Metaphor, Personification, Pathetic fallacy).				

TASK	EXAMPLE	QUOTATIONS	COMMENTS
Rhythm: movement, meter: arrangement of words and syllables, or feet, in a rhythmic pattern according to their length and stress; a particular pattern or scheme. Iambic pentameter? Does it sound like the subject? Does it change during the poem?			
Rhyme: pattern in the sound at the end of the line – e.g. rhyming couplets aa bb. Alternate rhyme scheme: abab. Limerick: aabba. English Sonnet: abab, cdcd, efef, gg. or Italian Sonnet: abba abba cddcdd, cdecde?			

TASK	EXAMPLE	QUOTATIONS	COMMENTS
Tone – Atmosphere and Mood: Humorous, Nonsense, Ironic Sad, Melancholic Romantic, tragic Eerie, Mysterious Dark, Ghostly Any other...			
Form – outward appearance: structure and organization. How many lines to a stanza (verse)? Effect of it shape Ballad, calligram, limerick, sonnet?			
Opinion: I think the poem is... because...			

Top Tip

Demonstrate how a poem should be read – to the punctuation, not the end of the line. Read it with the pupil, taking turns alternately changing over at each punctuation mark.

- Read the poem aloud to your target pupil, exaggerating the emotions of the text.

In pairs (A and B), read 'The Eagle' like this:

A A poem by Alfred,
B Lord Tennyson.
A 'The Eagle'.
B He clasps the crag with crooked hands;
A Close to the sun in lonely lands,
B Ring'd with the azure world,
A   he stands.
B The wrinkled sea beneath him crawls;
A He watches from his lonely walls,
B And like a thunderbolt he falls.

For younger pupils use the Understanding Poetry Template to support the pupil's comprehension.

Template 14.4 – Understanding Poetry

Paste the poem here

1. The poem is about ....

2. The poet's idea (theme) is..

3. The poet is writing about the feeling of ....

4. The sentences are long/short. The order of the words are ....

5. List your favourite words. Write why you like these words.

....

6. Similes: ....

Metaphors: ....

Alliteration: ....

Assonance: ....

7. How many syllables are there in each line? ....

8. Write out the rhymes scheme ....

9. What is the mood of the poem? ....

10. The poem is .... It has ..... lines in ... verses. It is a ....

11. I think the poem is.................................because ....

....

Writing poetry

Begin with concrete details of the subject, for example, describing an animal. Use pictures as a reference, for example, four photos of a cat: crouching in the grass, stalking its prey, leaping, and pouncing. The sequence can form the basis for a poem.

The My Poetry Template can be used to support poetry writing alongside illustration, or to explore simile and metaphor. Write the image (the trees stood like soldiers) on the lines. Ask the pupil to select the correct image from a choice of two pictures: 1) picture of soldiers on parade; 2) picture of trees planted in ranks to illustrate the meaning of the imagery.

Template 14.5 – My Poetry

Poem Title: ....

....
....
....
....

....
....
....
....

....
....
....
....

....
....
....
....

....
....
....
....

....
....
....
....

15 Science, Technologies and PE

Pupils with an ASC have a number of difficulties that may impact on their conduct and learning in these subjects.

Cognitive processing

- Hypothesizing and predicting before conducting an experiment or making something.
- Detailed focus processing (DFP) may mean that they focus on a part and do not get the bigger picture.
- Conversely – DFP may also mean that they will be able to see the detail and pick up mistakes or data others miss.
- Perfection – the need for perfection may inhibit their rate of progress or even stop them attempting a task they don't feel confident about.

Literacy

- A new vocabulary needs to be learned. What may mean one thing in everyday language may mean another in Science or Technology, for example, face could mean a side of an object, not the front part of a person's head from the forehead to the chin.

Sensory

- Pupils may have sensory difficulties dealing with practical subjects.
- Hypersensitive senses can result in an extreme reaction, for example, a hypersensitive sense of smell can lead to the pupil being sick in a science lesson. Or a hypersensitive sense of touch may mean the pupil cannot handle food or paints. Forcing a pupil with these hypersensitivities may lead to the pupil becoming distressed. However, you may find that the pupil enjoys the sensations on offer and covers their hand in paint or flour; or obsessively strokes a cloth or hammers wood.
- Hyposensitivity may cause issues regarding health and safety, for example, if the pupil is less sensitive to touch they may burn themselves.

Poor motor skills

- Practical subjects are difficult to do.
- Proprioception and vestibular difficulties may make the pupil clumsy when walking round the practical area.
- Handling equipment may be awkward and accidents are more likely to happen.
- Using unfamiliar tools and utensils may cause the pupil pain.
- Measuring exact amounts of a substance, for example, pouring water into a jug or a beaker may be difficult.

Organization

- There is a large amount of organization needed to prepare for and carry out the experiment, or produce the practical work, in Science and Technology. The array of equipment, tools and utensils are likely to be confusing, especially if there are different tools that do similar jobs.

Difficulties include:

1 Making a decision.
2 Knowing how to start.
3 Sustaining a piece of work.
4 Knowing how to finish it.

Rigid behaviour

This may result in the following:

- Lack of understanding that tools and equipment have multiple uses.
- Expectation that they will use exactly the same tools each lesson.
- Rigid interpretation of the rules may mean that if they are told not to touch something – they won't, ever. They are likely to adhere to the rules of the lab or tech room to the letter.
- Policing peers who 'bend' the rules.

Health and Safety

- Sensory issues may make wearing safety equipment, like goggles, intolerable.
- A pupil with an ASC may not be aware of the dangers of some procedures, equipment or materials being handled.

Strategies

Cognitive processing

- A hypothesis is a statement, which can be tested, e.g. plants need light to grow.
- Formalise it using the following:
  If I (grow a plant in a cupboard) **then** (it won't grow) **because** (it needs light to grow).
- Break down tasks using templates.
- Complete task one step at a time.
- Allow time for processing.
- Support with illustrations and diagrams.

Literacy

- Make up a key words list for each topic, with illustrations or symbols.
- Use a science dictionary.

Sensory

- Check for any sensory issues.
- Make reasonable adjustments: allow them to wear ear defenders in noisy lessons; wear plastic gloves in Food Technology when handling food.
- If the practical lesson is likely to be a major difficulty the pupil clearly cannot handle, give the pupil a job as record keeper.

Poor motor skills

- A TA should be assigned to support a pupil with dyspraxia in any practical lesson, to fetch the necessary tools and equipment. This will minimize the pupil's travel about a room or provide a helping hand when needed. Note: the pupil may not ask for help – be alert.
- Keep all the equipment needed to complete the task in a deep-sided plastic tray on the work area. Be prepared before the start of the lesson, or give the pupil the tray with an illustrated list of equipment they need to collect.
- Use equipment specially adjusted for weak grip and hypermobility, if necessary. The pupil may experience pain using the equipment for any length of time.

Organization

- Use a key fob for pre-lesson preparation as necessary:
  Get out/put on – list all equipment needed/instructions on a key fob.
- Place all equipment for the lesson into a deep-sided plastic tray.
- Or use an illustrated key fob list for gathering the equipment into a deep-sided tray.
- Include illustrated instructions for the practical task.
- Keep the text to a minimum. Word free, DIY instructions are the best.

- Include a diagram or photograph of the correct final set up of the equipment or finished product.
- One step at a time, that is, one step on one piece of paper.
- Tidying up – list what to do to clean up properly and where to put things away.
- Colour code equipment matching their storage areas.
- Hazards of conducting the practical should also be highlighted, using illustrations.

Rigid behaviour

- Demonstrate all the practical uses of the equipment.
- Some pupils may get upset if someone else is using 'their' equipment. Colour code 'their' equipment.
- Assign a workstation dedicated to all pupils with rigid behaviour, with a set of tools assigned to that workstation.
- Put together a group to work with the pupil, who are tolerant and understanding of their behaviour.

Health and Safety

- **Do not assume that the pupil will be able to infer from the task set what the hazards are.**
- Make sure the pupil understands the labels alerting what type of hazard the material presents.
- Place a laminated, illustrated list of hazards, associated with the task, into the tray.
- Ask the pupil to tell you what the hazards of doing the task are.
- Below is a link to a little game that will alert the pupil to the hazards of a science lab: http://www.interactivesolutions.co.uk/games/flashGames/labHazards.htm.

Science

Science is often one of the areas of strength for a pupil on the autism spectrum because it deals with facts and figures. Some of the world's greatest scientists, who developed their area of interest until they became super-specialists, have Asperger Syndrome. They never gave up, making discoveries that have, quite literally, changed the world. However, many scientists did not show this promise in school.

Learning the facts of science subjects may be relatively easy, being logical and governed by natural laws.

Strategies

- Use the following templates to support the pupil in Science experiments and other practical lessons.
- Apply the strategies outlined above.
- Divide the data collection box (see the template below) into the required number of sections needed for the experiment.

- Collect any graph data on a separate sheet of paper and staple the completed graph into the booklet when it has been completed.
- Record the data for the pupil with proprioception difficulties, or hypermobility. Use a sharp pencil to record the data.
- The last page of the template has been left blank for any additional diagram results.

Science Experiments Booklet

Name: ....

Form: ....

Subject: ....

Date: ....

Teacher: ....

Room: ....

Teacher's Comments

What you did well: ....

....

....

How to improve: ....

....

....

Evaluation

Think about – Equipment and Method.

I could have made my experiment better by:

....

....

....

....

....

....

....

Hypothesizing

A hypothesis is an idea I have about something based upon what I can sense (see, hear, smell, taste or feel).

I need to do an experiment to gather evidence to prove that my idea is correct.

Statement: ....

....

....

Therefore, if I ....

....

then.. will happen.

9

Diagram Results

Equipment List – I need:

```
...........    ...........
:          :   :
:          :   :
```

4

Observations: I see that

1. ....

Method: I will

1. ....

Diagram

Risk Assessment

Safety First

Hazard: ....

Risk: ....

Control: ....

Data - Results

	1	2	3	4

My Experiment

I want to find out: ....
....

I am going to: ....
....

INDEPENDENT VARIABLE – *change:*
....

DEPENDENT VARIABLE – *measure:*
....

CONTROL VARIABLE – *remains the same:*
....

Conclusions

I found that ....
....

My hypothesis/idea was/wasn't backed up by the results
because: ....
....
....
....

Technology and Art

The need for perfection may make practical subjects difficult for the pupil to carry out. They may become fixated on getting it absolutely right or, if they make a mistake, want to throw it away and start again.

While most of the aforementioned strategies may be applied to these subjects, they come with a different set of issues regarding health and safety.

- Ensure that you have the information to relay the dangers of the equipment used, with diagrams, in the tray.
- Whenever there are mechanical tools involved, especially electric tools, do not simply rely on diagrams to convey safety information.
- Ask the teacher to take the time to demonstrate how to use tools properly, highlighting the hazards as they do.
- Most workrooms have 'instructions for safe use' on a sign next to the relevant machinery; ensure that this is supplemented with diagrams. It would be helpful to show the risks in a diagram too.
- Make sure that the pupil has a list of materials needed stapled into their school planner, homework diary, or Comms Book – they may lose it or forget to inform their parents that they need to bring in materials for a lesson.
- Use this Practical 1 Template to focus their attention on what needs to be done.

Template 15.2 – Practical Subjects

Subject: ....

Task: (I have to) ....

....

....

I need: (Equipment)..

....

....

....

....

....

I am going to: (Method)..

....

....

....

....

....

....

At the end of the lesson I need to: ....

....

....

....

PE

This is a minefield for pupils with AS but is one of the most valuable subjects for learning a large variety of physical and social skills. Many pupils study martial arts and other individual sports outside school, but teamwork and being able to meet expectations in a noisy, boisterous environment may be very confusing and frustrating.

Difficulties

- Remembering and organizing PE kit.
- Getting changed – fine motor skills.
- Dyspraxia – gross motor skill deficit.
- Gym – acoustics, lack of awareness of personal space.
- Field – sensory overload, shouted instructions.
- Social interaction – identifying team members.
- Mind blindness – inability to read team mates' signals.
- Lack of anticipation.
- Lack of impulse control.
- Proprioception and vestibular difficulties.
- Peer intolerance.

Strategies

- Support the pupil at all times in changing rooms.
- Display instructions for changing into and out of PE kit.
- Teach games skills and rules of the game first.
- Individual sports or smaller team games are less stressful.
- Zero tolerance for any bullying.

16 School trips

School trips are great opportunities to expand life experiences and develop life skills. Good organization and planning are the key to any successful school trip. Pupils with AS will need to be carefully organized. Anxiety will be the overwhelming emotion – the fear of the unknown and the lack of control.

Once a letter home has been sent, contact the parents to check that they have received it and invite them into school to discuss the trip and how best you can help prepare the pupil together. Some pupils may be well travelled and need the minimum support.

Discuss their travel experience and the modes of transport they are familiar with. Find out their daily routines for getting up in the morning and going to bed at night, relaxation techniques, food, sensory issues, phobias, use of public conveniences, sharing a room. The pupil's family may have tried and tested travel routines and be able to give advice on any potential difficulties.

Apply routines already used by parents. Keep everything as predictable as possible. If there are strategies used by parents to reduce anxiety levels – audio or games devices, puzzle books or sketch or note pads, use them. If possible, give them their own room: they will need to have their own space and time to unwind. If this is not practical, ensure that the person/s sharing with the pupil is a buddy and tolerant of the need for down time and prepared to give them some space. Taking their own duvet and pillow may help them settle.

The level of differentiation depends on how competent or how anxious the pupil is. The main thing is to ensure that the pupil with AS feels safe and knows what to expect. The level of scaffolding may be reduced after negotiation if you feel the pupil is managing the trip well.

Strategies

Before the trip

1   Assign the key TA to the pupil several weeks in advance to prepare for the trip.
2   If the key TA can also accompany the pupil on the trip to help monitor and manage the child, this would be ideal. A trusted member of staff that the pupil knows will be there to help at all times, will relieve the stress.
3   The key TA should discuss with the pupil what is likely to cause stress and how to alleviate it.
4   Familiarization – pay attention to any new experiences. If the pupil has never been away from home before, it would be useful for their parents to give them the experience of visiting a hotel and sharing a room. If giving the pupil their own room on the trip is not going to be practical ensure that they share with a trusted peer, who is tolerant and supportive
5   Practise long distance travel on a coach and visiting service stations during stopovers to use the toilets or get a snack.

6   The pupil will need to be told what to expect when they reach the airport/ferry terminal and on the aircraft/ferry. If the airport/ferry terminal is nearby, it may be helpful for the parents to take them on a preliminary visit.

7   Create a School Trip booklet with the pupil. Include space for a diary and recording anything to do with their special interest that they may find on the trip: birds and insects, foreign number plates and makes of cars, postcards and stamps.

8   A list of things to pack for a residential trip and any special equipment needed should be sent home. Ask the parents to have a checklist of all the pupil's belongings on a spreadsheet so that they can keep track of them if they are staying in several different locations.

9   Have the pupil pack a daysack or small bag to carry during the journey, with copies of travel documents and other papers in a plastic, zipped envelope, wallet/purse, snack, drink, books, puzzles and audio or games devices to help distract them.

10   Outline what to do in an emergency, such as locking themselves out of the hotel room. Write a list of concise instructions to help the pupil feel more secure.

11   Assign a couple of carefully selected buddies to support the pupil. Check they are acceptable to the pupil.

12   Discuss food options with the parents. Generally speaking, basic foods: plain meat and potatoes, pizza and pasta will be acceptable.

13   Rules should be clear and concise. Explain what behaviour you expect and why. These may also be written down.

14   Describe and discuss the physical signs of distress that the pupil may feel when anxious. Give the pupil strategies to monitor these and how to calm themselves and at what point help should be sought.

15   Discreet signals should also be arranged for the pupil to indicate levels of stress to staff members or trusted buddies who know them well.

16   Take the pupil through the itinerary. Discuss and agree what to do should the pupil become anxious. This is especially important if a TA is not specifically assigned to support the pupil throughout the day.

17   Exchange mobile phone numbers and ensure that enough credit is on the pupil's phone for the trip.

18   Check instructions for the dispensing of any medication.

19   Agree a time to contact parents. The pupil may need to speak to parents regularly. Be aware that the parents will also be anxious and would appreciate a call from you to reassure them all is well.

Maps

1   When using a single map for the whole trip, trace arrowed routes in different colours for different days.

2   Itinerary – supplement the map with a timeline including dates, times and places, using as few words as possible.

3   Use approximate timings: ETD (estimated time of departure) 0900–0930 and ETA (estimated time of arrival). Potential for delay should be explained. Use an analogue clock with the approximate time shaded.

4   Use illustrations of key sites such as airports, ferry terminals, hotel, tourist sights, ruins and museums.

5   Plot the order of sites to be visited on a daily itinerary using numbers, with different colours for mornings and afternoons. Directional arrows may be helpful.

6   Include maps of large sites and a pre-arranged meeting point and a rendezvous time.

During the trip

1   Arrive at the departure point before the pupil to greet them and distract them should there be any delay.

2   Retain original documents and give out spending money, as needed, for the day. Poor organizational skills may result in the pupil losing their passport, tickets and money. Have different purses for different currencies.

3   Documents in their daysack should include an autism alert card (translated into the language of the country being visited or travelled through), staff name and mobile telephone number, school telephone number and name of the travel company. These should be self-explanatory to the authorities because, faced with a crisis, the pupil may not be able to communicate effectively.

4   Do not deviate from arrangements agreed with the pupil unless you have discussed and agreed any change beforehand.

5   Monitor mood and reactions carefully but don't be overly fussy. If you have done your preparation well, then the pupil will know what to do in any eventuality.

6   Develop the pupil's independence: arrange to meet at regular intervals at pre-arranged rendezvous points throughout the day.

7   Set reminder alarms on the pupil's mobile phone. Note on the itinerary: where, when, who...

8   Do not make food an issue by drawing attention to any idiosyncrasies associated with it. Respect the pupil's choice even if it is exactly the same meal every day. It may be the only thing they can control. The need for sameness may be the need for predictability and security.

9   Unstructured leisure time may be difficult for the pupil. Do not force them to participate in a sporting event or go to a disco. They will need time to recharge after a day of new experiences. They may prefer to fill in their trip diary or simply be alone for a time playing on a portable gaming device.

10   Enjoy the trip and the new perspective your pupil with AS will give you!

Afterword

I set out writing these books because I saw that many of us involved in education needed to understand why we had to make 'big' adjustments for the pupil with an ASC.

The ability of our children with an ASC to go on to manage in secondary schools is largely down to your tolerance and tenacity. Your challenges are greater, in that our children come to you when they are struggling to manage themselves and adapt to a bigger society.

Sadly, life becomes considerably more difficult for our children when they go into secondary schools. The support for their complex needs is often diluted in the pursuit of examination results. What resilience they have is bound up in the belief in themselves that you have given them, together with the support of their parents. With your support our children do the most extraordinary things.

They need understanding, tolerance and all the support you can give them to be accepted and respected for who they are, to survive in school, develop skills and achieve, so that they may have a rewarding future and contribute to society.

It is my hope that you will take the ideas in this book and develop your own strategies to support your Asperkids to access the curriculum and join in the communal life of the school and the community for a long time to come.

Glossary

Definitions of Autism Spectrum Conditions are taken from the National Autistic Society webpage: http://www.autism.org.uk/About-autism/All-about-diagnosis/Jargon-buster/Glossary-of-terms-a.aspx.

Other definitions are mostly taken from the online *Oxford Dictionary of British English* (http://oxforddictionaries.com).

ABC chart: chart used to analyze incidents to effect better outcomes in the future.
- **A**ntecedent – what happened leading up to the problem behaviour.
- **B**ehaviour – the observed problem behaviour.
- **C**onsequence – the event that immediately follows the response.

Affective empathy: able to feel physically what others are feeling.

Alliteration: the occurrence of the same letter or sound at the beginning of adjacent or closely connected words (e.g. big blue balloon).

Allusion: an expression designed to call something to mind without mentioning it explicitly; an indirect or passing reference.

Amygdala: a roughly almond-shaped mass of grey matter inside each cerebral hemisphere, involved with the experiencing of emotions.

Anaphoric cueing: using the pronoun to refer to the noun that precedes it.

Asperger Syndrome (AS): An autism spectrum condition that affects the way a person communicates and relates to others. A number of traits of autism are common to Asperger Syndrome, including:
- difficulty in communicating
- difficulty in social relationships
- a lack of imagination and creative play.

People with Asperger Syndrome usually have fewer problems with language than those with autism, often speaking fluently though their words can sometimes sound formal or stilted. People with Asperger Syndrome also do not have the accompanying learning disabilities often associated with autism; in fact, people with Asperger Syndrome are often of average or above average intelligence (NAS).

Asperkid: an affectionate term for a child with Asperger Syndrome.

Assonance: resemblance of sound between syllables of nearby words, arising particularly from the rhyming of two or more stressed vowels, but not consonants (e.g. how now brown cow), but also from the use of identical consonants with different vowels (e.g. killed, cold, culled).

AS Unit: special unit in school designed to meet the needs of pupils with Asperger Syndrome or an Autism Spectrum Unit.

Auditory or aural: sense of hearing.

Autism Spectrum Condition (ASC): a broad range of lifelong, neurological physiological conditions, which affects the way people behave and interact with the world socially, sensorially, and by their use of language and lack of flexibility.

Autism also known as **Kanner's Syndrome/Classic** autism or **Low Functioning Autism (LFA):** a lifelong developmental disability that affects the way a person communicates and relates to people around them. Children and adults with autism are unable to relate to others in a meaningful way. Their ability to develop friendships is impaired, as is their capacity to understand other people's feelings. All people with autism have impairments in social interactions, social communication and imagination. This is referred to as the triad of impairments. (NAS)

Avoidance behaviour: avoidance by a pupil with autism of the everyday demands made by other people, due to their high anxiety levels when they feel that they are not in control (NAS).

Backhanded bullying: where a pupil with AS is misled to do something inappropriate thereby getting them into trouble.

Bombmeter: a 0–10, emotional assessment tool in the shape of a thermometer with the spectrum rising to red.

Caesura: a pause near the middle of a line of poetry.

CATS DIRRT FO: mnemonic to remember what to include in poetry analysis.

Cerebral hemisphere: each of the two parts of the cerebrum (left and right) in the brain of a vertebrate: the left hemisphere plays a dominant role in the comprehension of language.

Cerebrum: the part of the brain located in the front area of the skull and consisting of two hemispheres, left and right, separated by a fissure. It is responsible for the integration of complex sensory and neural functions and the initiation and coordination of voluntary activity in the body.

Cognitive empathy: being able to recognize how others are feeling, without feeling it.

Comic Conversations: comic strip conversations are visual representations of the different levels of communication that happen in a conversation. Devised by Carol Gray (NAS).

Compare and contrast: compare: similarities; contrast: differences.

Declarative language: describes what it wants to accomplish rather than focusing on how to achieve that goal.

Dendrite: (Physiology) a short-branched extension of a nerve cell, along which impulses received from other cells at synapses are transmitted to the cell body.

Detail Focus Processing: to focus on details, disregarding the whole.

Dialogue: a conversation between two or more people as a feature of a book, play, or film.

Diction: the choice and use of words and phrases in speech or writing.

Differentiation: presenting educational material to pupils in different formats and methods to enable them to make sense of it and process it so that they can learn effectively, regardless of differences in ability and learning styles.

DSM-IV: Diagnostic and Statistical Manual of Mental Disorders, the American Psychiatric Association's (APA) diagnostic reference book now replaced by DSM 5 (May 2013).

Dyslexia: disorders that involve difficulty in learning to read or interpret words, letters, and other symbols, but that do not affect general intelligence.

Dyspraxia: impairment or immaturity of the organization of movement with associated problems of language, perception and thought (NAS).

Echolalia: repetition of another person's spoken words as a means of communication in autism.

Egocentric: thinking only of oneself, without regard for the feelings or desires of others.

Enjambment: the continuation of a sentence without a pause beyond the end of a line, couplet, or stanza.

Executive Function: the ability to plan and carry out complex cognitive tasks. In autism this ability is interfered with by dysfunction in the frontal lobes of the brain. (Trevarthen *et al.*, *Children with Autism*) (NAS). EF deficit includes a poor working memory, inattention, and difficulties initiating, sustaining and inhibiting actions.

Executive Functioning Skills: organizational skills.

Exit card: a small card given to pupils with special needs. The pupil shows it to the teacher when they have to leave the lesson.

FERB: Functional Equivalent Replacement Behaviour.

Figurative language: departing from a literal use of words.

Fine motor skills: using the smaller muscles that are used to pick up and manipulate small objects, to write, and to fasten clothing.

fMRI scans: functional magnetic resonance imaging scans, which detect blood flow through the brain and are used to measure the brain's response to stimuli in experiments conducted to find out how the brain operates.

Form: the visible shape or configuration of a poem.

Frontal cerebral cortex: the outer layer of the cerebrum (the cerebral cortex) at the front of the brain, composed of folded grey matter and playing an important role in consciousness.

Frontal lobe: each of the paired lobes of the brain lying immediately behind the forehead, including areas concerned with behaviour, learning, personality, and voluntary movement.

GAPS: in factual essay writing, consider Genre (type of writing), Audience, Purpose and Style of writing.

Glycine: amino acid that is present in blood platelets and serum, which acts as a neurotransmitter.

Graphic novel/play: novels and plays in cartoon form.

Grey matter: the darker tissue of the brain and spinal cord, consisting mainly of nerve cell bodies and branching dendrites.

Gross motor skills: using the larger muscles that are used to walk, jump, run and general movement in sports.

Gustatory: sense of taste.

Heterogeneous: diverse in character – in autism this means that no two people share the same characteristics, therefore each person with autism presents differently with the condition.

High stakes examinations: examinations that impact upon your future studies and career choices.

Hippocampus: the centre of emotion, memory and the unconscious nervous system.

Homographs: words that are *spelt* the same but have different meanings.

Homonyms: words that are *spelt* the same but have different meanings; words with double meanings.

Homophones: words that are *spelt* differently, *pronounced* the same, but have different meanings.

Hyperbole: exaggeration.

Hyperlexia: being able to read (from a very early age, in some cases) without really understanding what you have read.

Hypermobility: particularly supple and able to move your limbs into positions others find impossible. Those with the condition may have a degree of low muscle tone and suffer from joint pain, back pain and be prone to dislocated joints and soft tissue injuries.

Hypersensitive: having an extreme physical sensitivity to particular substances or conditions.

Hyposensitive: having a reduced sensitivity to particular substances or conditions.

Hypothalamus: a region of the forebrain that coordinates both the involuntary or unconscious nervous system and the activity controlling body temperature, thirst, hunger and involved in sleep and emotional activity.

Iambic pentameter: rhythm shown by 5 metric feet di dah (short long) -/-/-/-/-/.

ICD-10: World Health Organization's International Classification of Diseases. The European reference book for medical professionals to consult when making a diagnosis.

Idiom: an expression of a given language that is peculiar to itself grammatically or cannot be understood from the individual meanings of its elements.

Idiomatic language: the language we use every day, rich in local expressions and sayings.

Idiosyncratic behaviour: strange behaviour peculiar to the individual.

Imagery: visually descriptive or figurative language, especially in a literary work.

Inference: the conclusion arrived at based upon available evidence.

Inset day: In Service Training Day for school staff.

Intervention: action taken to improve a situation.

Irony: the expression of one's meaning by using language that normally signifies the opposite, typically for humorous or emphatic effect.

Kanner Syndrome/classic autism: neural developmental disorder characterized by impaired social interaction and verbal and non-verbal communication, and by restricted, repetitive or stereotyped behaviour. The diagnostic criteria require symptoms to be apparent before a child is three years old.

Key fob: laminated aide memoires on a key ring to remind the pupil what to do in any given situation. Colour code to task.

Key Stages: ages at which a pupil is expected to achieve a certain academic standard.

Key words: the words associated with a topic being studied, or the words in an essay title or question, which tell the reader exactly what they have to do.

Literal interpretation: taking words in their usual or most basic sense without metaphor or exaggeration; words that do not deviate from their defined meaning.

Litotes: understatement.

Meltdown: an uncontrolled emotional outburst that is a neurological response to stress or sensory overload.

Metaphor: a figure of speech in which a word or phrase is applied to an object or action to which it is not literally applicable (e.g. he is a lion).

Metre: a unit of measurement or the rhythm of a poem.

Mnemonic: a system such as a pattern of letters, ideas, or associations, which assists in remembering something.

Myelin: a whitish insulating sheath around many nerve fibres, which increases the speed at which impulses are conducted.

Narration: a character tells the story.

NAS: National Autistic Society, UK charity for people with autism.

Neural: relating to a nerve or the nervous system: patterns of neural activity.

Neuron: a specialized cell transmitting nerve impulses; a nerve cell.

Neuro-physiological disorder: a condition brought about by natural differences in formation of the brain, which cause difficulties in processing.

Neurotransmitter: a chemical substance that is released at the end of a nerve fibre by the arrival of a nerve impulse and, by diffusing across the synapse or junction, effects the transfer of the impulse to another nerve fibre, a muscle fibre, or some other structure.

Neuro Typical (NT): term coined by the autistic community to refer to those not on the Autism Spectrum.

Olfactory: sense of smell.

Onomatopoeia: the formation of a word from a sound associated with what is named (e.g. cuckoo, sizzle).

Opinion: a view or judgement formed about something, not necessarily based on fact or knowledge.

Pathetic fallacy: the attribution of human feelings and responses to inanimate things or animals, especially in art and literature.

Pathological demand avoidance: an autism spectrum disorder where individuals resist and avoid the ordinary demands of life, using skilful strategies that are socially manipulative (distracting adults, using excuses, appearing to become physically incapacitated). (A. Worthington (ed.), *Fulton Special Education Digest*) (NAS).

PEEL (Point Evidence Explanation Link): method for focusing pupil's attention on the content of a factual or critical essay written in response to a question for coursework or examination.

Peer intervention: action taken with peers of the pupils with AS to improve a situation or the relationship between them.

Persona (personae – plural): the main character in a poem.

Personification: the attribution of a personal nature or human characteristics to something non-human, or the representation of an abstract quality in human form. A figure intended to represent an abstract quality.

Pervasive developmental disorder not otherwise specified (PDD-NOS): disorders which fit the general description for pervasive developmental disorders, but in which contradictory findings or lack of adequate information mean that the criteria for other pervasive developmental disorders cannot be met (ICD10) (NAS).

Pica: a tendency to eat substances other than normal food.

Proprioception: sense of movement and the awareness of the body in space, position.

Psychiatry: the study and treatment of mental illness, emotional disturbance and abnormal behaviour.

Psychology: the scientific study of the human mind and its functions, especially those affecting behaviour in a given context. An Educational Psychologist specializes in the context of education.

Pun: a joke exploiting the different possible meanings of a word or the fact that there are words that sound alike but have different meanings.

Pupil Passport: document outlining information about the individual, useful to all school staff.

Pupil Referral Unit: local authority establishments that provide education for children unable to attend a mainstream school.

Retts Syndrome: a profoundly disabling neurological disorder that only affects girls. A slowing of development and regression, with loss of skills in speech and hand use and social withdrawal, begins at around one to three years. Motor development is severely impaired, with difficulty in planning and coordinating movement (NAS).

Rhetoric: the art of effective or persuasive speaking or writing, especially the exploitation of figures of speech and other compositional techniques.

Rhetorical question: asked in order to produce an effect or to make a statement rather than to elicit information.

Rhyme: correspondence of sound between words or the endings of words, especially when these are used at the ends of lines of poetry.

Rhythm: the measured flow of words and phrases in verse or prose as determined by the relation of long and short or stressed and unstressed syllables.

Role: stepping into another character's shoes.

Role model: someone the pupil with AS can identify with and admire.

Sarcasm: the use of irony to mock or convey contempt.

Satire: the use of humour, irony, exaggeration or ridicule to expose and criticize people's stupidity or vices, particularly in the context of contemporary politics and other topical issues.

Savant: a person with a learning disability who has pool(s) of extraordinary ability.

Scribe: to write for the pupil.

SEN register: list of pupils with a Special Educational Need in the school.

SENCo (Special Educational Needs Co-ordinator): head of SEN Department in school.

Sensory Box: a (shoe) box with items used to stimulate or soothe the senses.

Sensory break: time out from the school 'day' to either calm down or stimulate a sense.

Sensory overload: the sensation becomes unbearable and the brain shuts down or goes into meltdown.

Sensory Room: a room filled with sensory tools to soothe or alert the senses for the pupil who needs a sensory snack during a sensory break.

Sensory snack: an activity done in the sensory break to soothe or alert the senses.

Serotonin: a compound present in blood platelets and serum that acts as a neurotransmitter.

Shutdown: where the body shuts down and the individual is unable to respond due to overload or stress.

Sibilance: a hissing sound.

Simile: a figure of speech comparing one thing with another thing of a different kind, making a description more emphatic or vivid; using the word 'like' or 'as' (e.g. as brave as a lion).

Social stories: used to teach social skills to people with autism. They are short descriptions of a particular situation, event or activity that include specific information about what to expect in that situation and why. Devised by Carol Gray (NAS).

Spectrum: a wide range.

Stanza: a verse in poetry.

Stim: (verb) short for indulging in self-stimulatory behaviours; (noun) a stimulatory behaviour.

Strategy: a plan of action designed to achieve a long-term or overall aim.

Symbol: 1) a thing that represents or stands for something else, especially a material object representing something abstract; 2) a mark or character used as a conventional representation of an object, function, or process, e.g. the letter or letters standing for a chemical element or a character in musical notation.

Symbolism: 1) the use of symbols to represent ideas or qualities; 2) an artistic and poetic movement or style using symbolic images and indirect suggestion to express mystical ideas, emotions, and states of mind.

Synapse: a junction between two nerve cells, consisting of a minute gap across which impulses pass by diffusion of a neurotransmitter.

Syntax: the arrangement of words and phrases to create well-formed sentences in a language.

TA: Teaching Assistant aka LSA.

Tactile: sense of touch.

Theme: an idea that recurs in or pervades a work of art or literature.

Theory of Mind (ToM): a philosophical concept of the understanding one has that another person has an individual perspective on states of affairs, that this consciousness depends in part on information that they may have which is not available to oneself and vice versa. (Trevarthen *et al.*, *Children with Autism*) (NAS).

Timeline: a line representing a period of time, on which important events are marked.

Tone: the general character or attitude/mood of a place, piece of writing, situation.

Tourette Syndrome: characterized by multiple tics characteristically involving the facial area (twitches, blinking, nodding), as well as phonic (vocal) tics. The onset of symptoms usually occurs between the ages of 2 and 21 (NAS).

Transition: moving from one place to another: primary to secondary school, or lesson in room 1 to lesson in room 7.

Vestibular: to do with sense of balance.

White matter: the paler tissue of the brain and spinal cord, consisting mainly of nerve fibres with their myelin sheaths.

Workmat: sheet of A3 paper with key words, symbols and pictures to illustrate the content of the lesson.

World knowledge: the knowledge gained through life experiences of interaction with one's environment, objects, life events, and other people.

Bibliography

Adair, R. and Norfolk County Council (2009). Disruptive Behaviour Checklist. http://www.schools.norfolk. gov.uk/Behaviour-and-safety/Behaviour/index.htm. Retrieved from the Internet, 25 June 2014.

Ambitious About Autism, Stats and Facts: http://www.ambitiousaboutautism.org.uk/page/about_autism/ stats_and_facts/index.cfm. Retrieved from the Internet, 16 December 2013.

APA (1994). *Diagnostic and Statistical Manual of Mental Disorders*, Fourth Edition (DSM IV). Washington, DC: American Psychiatric Association.

Attwood, T. (2006). *The Complete Guide to Asperger Syndrome.* London: Jessica Kingsley Publishers.

Barnard, J., Prior, A. and Potter, D. (2001). *Inclusion and Autism: is it working*? London: The National Autistic Society.

Baron-Cohen, S. (2008). *The Facts: Autism and Asperger Syndrome*. Oxford: Oxford University Press.

Baron-Cohen, S., Scott, F.J., Allison, C., Williams, J., Bolton, P., Matthews, F.E. and Carol Brayne, C. (2009). Prevalence of autism-spectrum conditions: UK school-based population study. *British Journal of Psychiatry*, 194: 500–9.

Beeman, M.J. and Bowden, E.M. (2000). Right and left hemispherical cooperation for drawing predictive and coherent inferences during normal story comprehension. *Brain and Language,* 71: 310–36.

Bogdashina, O. (2005). *Communication Issues in Autism and Asperger Syndrome. Do we speak the same language?* London: Jessica Kingsley Publishers.

—— (2006). *Theory of Mind and the Triad of Perspectives on Autism and Asperger Syndrome: a view from the bridge*. London: Jessica Kingsley Publishers.

—— (2010). *Autism and the Edges of the Known World: sensitivities, language and constructed reality*. London: Jessica Kingsley Publishers.

Church, C., Alisanski, S. and Amanullah, S. (2000). The social, behavioural, and academic experience of children with Asperger Syndrome. *Focus on Autism and Other Developmental Disabilities*, 15: 12–20.

Clements, J. and Zarkowska, E. (1994). *Problem Behaviour and People with Severe Learning Disabilities: the S.T.A.R. approach*. London: Chapman and Hall.

—— (2000). *Behavioural Concerns and Autistic Spectrum Disorders: explanations and strategies for change*. London: Jessica Kingsley Publishers.

Connelly, M. (2004). *Children with Autism Strategies for Accessing the Curriculum Key Stages 3 and 4*. Blackpool: North West Regional SEN Partnership.

Cumine, V., Dunlop, J. and Stevenson, G. (2010 second edition). *Asperger Syndrome: a practical guide for teachers*. Abingdon: Routledge (first published 1998; London: David Fulton).

Dowd, S. (2010). *The London Eye Mystery*. London: David Fickling Books.

Dubin, N. (2007). *Asperger Syndrome and Bullying Strategies and Solutions*. London: Jessica Kingsley Publishers.

Duffy, F.H., Shankardass, A., McAnulty, G.B. and Al, A. (2013). The relationship of Asperger's syndrome to autism: a preliminary EEG coherence study. *BMC Medicine*, 11: 175 doi:10.1186/1741-7015-11-175.

Elvén, B.H. (2010). *No fighting, No biting, No screaming. How to make behaving positively possible for people with autism and other developmental disabilities*. London: Jessica Kingsley Publishers.

Fisher, A.V., Karrie E., Godwin, K.E. and Seltman, H. (2014). Visual environment, attention allocation, and learning in young children: when too much of a good thing may be bad. *Psychological Science*.

Published in Science Daily, 27 May 2014. www.sciencedaily.com/releases/2014/05/140527100646. htm. Retrieved from Internet, 30 May 2014.

Frith, U. (2003). *Autism: explaining the enigma*. 2nd edition. Oxford: Wiley-Blackwell.

Frith, U. and Snowling, M. (1983). Reading for meaning and reading for sound in autistic and dyslexic children. *British Journal of Developmental Psychology*, 1(4): 329–42.

Gernsbacher, M.A. and Robertson, R. (1999). The role of suppression in figurative language comprehension. *Journal of Pragmatics*, 31: 1619–30.

Glenndenning, J. (2008/2009). Statistical First Release, Key Stage 4 Attainment by Pupil Characteristics, in England. http://www.education.gov.uk/rsgateway/DB/SFR/s000900/index.shtml. Retrieved 5 May 2012.

Gold, R., Faust M. and Goldstein, A. (2010). Semantic integration during metaphor comprehension in Asperger syndrome. *Brain and Language,*113: 124–34.

Gray, C. (1994). *Comic Strip Conversations: Illustrated interactions that teach conversation skills to students with autism and related disorders*. Texas: Future Horizons.

Griswold, D.E., Barnhill, G.P., Myles, B.S., Hagiwara, T. and Simpson, R.L. (2002). Asperger syndrome and academic achievement. *Focus on Autism and Other Developmental Disabilities*, 17: 94–102.

Haddon, M. (2004). *The Curious Incident of the Dog in the Night Time*. (Children's Edition) Vintage Reprints edition.

Hala, S., Pexman, P.M. and Glenwright, M. (2007). Priming the meaning of homographs in typically developing children and children with autism. *Journal of Autism and Developmental Disorders*, 36(1): 5–25.

Happé, F. and Frith, U. (2006). The weak coherence account: detail-focused cognitive style in autism spectrum disorders. *Journal of Autism and Developmental Disorders*, 36(1): 5–25..

Heinrichs, R. (2003). *Perfect Targets: Asperger Syndrome and bullying – practical solutions for surviving the social world*. Kansas: Autism Asperger Publishing Co.

Henderson, L.M., Clarke, P.J. and Snowling, M.J. (2011). Accessing and selecting word meaning in autism spectrum disorder. *Journal of Child Psychology and Psychiatry*, 52(9): 964–73.

Hesmondhalgh, M. (2006). *Access and Inclusion on the Front Line*. London: Jessica Kingsley Publishers.

Huemer, S.V. and Mann, V. (2010). A comprehensive profile of decoding and comprehension in autism spectrum disorders. *Journal of Autism and Developmental Disorders*, 40: 485–93.

Humphrey, N. and Symes, W. (2011). Peer interaction patterns among adolescents with autistic spectrum disorders (ASDs) in mainstream school settings. *Autism,*15(4): 397–419.

Humphrey, N. (2012). Inclusion of Pupils with Autistic Spectrum Disorders in Mainstream Secondary Schools – Challenges and Opportunities; ESRC Impact Report, RES-061-25-0054. Swindon: ESRC.

Jackson, L. (2003). *Freaks, Geeks and Asperger Syndrome*. London: Jessica Kingsley Publishers.

Jolliffe, T. and Baron-Cohen, S. (1999). A test of central coherence theory: linguistic processing in high-functioning adults with autism or Asperger syndrome: is local coherence impaired? *Cognition*, 71: 149–85.

Jones, G., English, A., Guldberg, K., Jordan, R., Richardson, R. and Waltz, M. (2009). *Educational provision for children and young people on the autism spectrum living in England: a review of current practice, issues and challenges*. London: Autism Education Trust.

Jordan, D. (2006) Functional Behavioral Assessment and Positive Interventions: What Parents Need to Know. http://www.pathfindersforautism.org/docs/Functional-Behavioral-Assessment-and-Positive-Interventions-(English).pdf, Retrieved 20 June 2014.

Joseph, R.M. and Tager-Flusberg, H. (2004). The relationship of theory of mind and executive functions to symptom type and severity in children with autism. *Development and Psychopathology,* 16: 137–55.

Jung-Beeman, M. (2005). Bilateral brain processes for comprehending natural language. *Trends in Cognitive Sciences*, 9: 512–18.

Just, M.A., Cherkassky, V.L., Keller, T.A. and Minshew, N.J. (2004). Cortical activation and synchronization during sentence comprehension in high-functioning autism: evidence of underconnectivity. *Brain*, 127: 1811–21.

Kaland, N., Møller-Nielsen, A., Smith, L., Mortensen, E.L., Callesen, K. and Gottlieb, D. (2005). The Strange Stories test. A replication study of children and adolescents with Asperger syndrome. *European Child and Adolescent Psychiatry*, 14: 73–82.

Kana, R.K., Keller, T.A., Minshew, N.J. and Just, M.A. (2007). Inhibitory control in high-functioning autism: decreased activation and underconnectivity in inhibition networks. *Biological Psychiatry,* 14: 73–82.

Kim, C. (2013). A Cognitive Defense of Stimming (or Why "Quiet Hands" Makes Math Harder). http://musingsofanaspie.com/2013/06/18/a-cognitive-defense-of-stimming-or-why-quiet-hands-makes-math-harder/ Retrieved 3 July 2013.

Lawson, W. (2000). *Life Behind Glass: a personal account of autism spectrum disorder*. London: Jessica Kingsley Publishers.

—— (2011). *The Passionate Mind: how people with autism learn.* London: Jessica Kingsley Publishers.

Le Sourn-Bissaoui, S., Caillies, S., Gierski, F. and Motte, J. (2011). Ambiguity detection in adolescents with Asperger syndrome: is central coherence or theory of mind impaired? *Research in Autism Spectrum Disorders*, 5: 648–56.

Loukusa, S., Leinonen, E., Jussila, K., Mattila, M-L., Ryder, N., Ebeling, H. and Moilanen, I. (2007). Answering contextually demanding questions: pragmatic errors produced by children with Asperger syndrome or high functioning autism. *Journal of Communication Disorders*, 40: 357–81.

Lyons, V. and Fitzgerald, M. (2004). Humor in Autism and Asperger Syndrome. *Journal of Autism and Developmental Disorders*, 34(5): 521–32.

Markram, H., Rinaldi, T. and Markram, K. (2007). The Intense World Syndrome – an alternative hypothesis for autism. *Frontiers in Neuroscience*, (1)1. www.frontiersin.org. Retrieved 28 December 2013.

Mashal, N., Faust, M., Hendler, T. and Jung-Beeman, M. (2008). Hemispheric differences in processing the literal interpretation of idioms: Converging evidence from behavioural and fMRI studies. *Cortex*, 10: 1016, cortex xxx, 1–13.

Mashal, N. and Kasirer, A. (2012). Principal component analysis study of visual and verbal metaphoric comprehension in children with autism and learning disabilities. *Research in Developmental Disabilities*, 33: 274–82.

Martin, I. and McDonald, S. (2004). An exploration of causes of non-literal language problems in individuals with Asperger Syndrome. *Journal of Autism and Developmental Disorders*, 34(3): 311–28.

McGlone, F., Wessberg, J. and Olausson, H. (2014). Discriminative and affective touch: sensing and feeling. *Neuron,* 82(4): 737–55. doi: 10.1016/j.neuron.2014.05.001.

Morewood, G.D., Humphrey, N. and Symes, W. (2011). Mainstreaming autism: making it work. *Good Autism Practice*, 12(2): 62–8.

Myles, B.S., Cook, K.T., Miller, N.E., Rinner, L. and Robbins, L.A. (2005 reprint). *Asperger Syndrome and Sensory Issues: practical solutions for making sense of the world*. Kansas: Autism Asperger Publishing Co.

Nation, K. and Norbury, C.F. (2005). Why reading comprehension fails insights from developmental disorders. *Topics in Language Disorders*, 25(1): 21–32.

Norbury, C.F. (2005). The relationship between theory of mind and metaphor: Evidence from children with language impairment and autistic spectrum disorder. *British Journal of Developmental Psychology*, 23: 383–99.

O'Connor, I.M. and Klein, P.D. (2004). Exploration of strategies for facilitating the reading comprehension of high-functioning students with Autism Spectrum Disorders. *Journal of Autism and Developmental Disorders*, 34(2): 115–26.

Pellicano, E., Maybery, M., Durkin, K. and Maley, A. (2006). Multiple cognitive capabilities deficits in children with an autism spectrum disorder: "weak" central coherence and its relationship to theory of mind and executive control. *Development and Psychopathology*, 18: 77–98.

Picoult, J. (2010). *House Rules*. London: Hodder Paperbacks.

Reid, B. and Batten, A. (2006). *B is for bullied: the experiences of children with autism and their families*. London: The National Autistic Society.

Riley-Hall, E. (2012). *Parenting Girls on the Autism Spectrum: overcoming the challenges and celebrating the gifts*. London: Jessica Kingsley Publishers.

Sainsbury, C. (2003). *Martian in the Playground*. London: Sage Publications Inc.

Saldaña, D. and Frith, U. (2007). Do readers with autism make bridging inferences from world knowledge? *Journal of Experimental Child Psychology,* 96: 310–19.

Saldaña, D., Carreiras, M. and Frith, U. (2009). Orthographic and phonological pathways in hyperlexic readers with autism spectrum disorders. *Developmental Neuropsychology*, 33(3): 240–53.

Shakespeare, W. (1606). *Macbeth* – The Graphic Novel: Original Text (2008). (Unabridged, British English) John McDonald (Adapter), Karen Wenborn (Collaborator), Nigel Dobbyn (Colorist), Jo Wheeler (Designer), Clive Bryant (Editor), Jon Haward (Illustrator), Gary Erskine (Illustrator) Classical Comics; British English edition.

Silver, K. (2005). *Assessing and Developing Communication and Thinking Skills in People with Autism and Communication Difficulties. A toolkit for parents and professionals*. London: Jessica Kingsley Publishers.

Simone, R. (2010). *Aspergirls: Empowering Females with Asperger Syndrome*. London: Jessica Kingsley Publishers.

Songlee, D., Miller, S.P., Tincani, M., Sileo, N.M. and Perkins, P.G. (2008). Effects of test-taking strategy instruction on high-functioning adolescents with autism spectrum disorders. *Focus on Autism and Other Developmental Disabilities*, 23: 217–28.

Stobart, A. (2009). *Bullying and autism spectrum disorders: a guide for school staff*. London: The National Autistic Society.

Supekar, K., Uddin, L.Q., Khouzam, A., Phillips, J., Gaillard, W.D., Kenworthy, L.E., Yerys, B.E., Vaidya, C.J. and Menon, V. (2013). Brain hyperconnectivity in children with autism and its links to social deficits, *Cell Press Open Access*. http://download.cell.com/cell-reports/mmcs/journals/2211-1247/PIIS22111 24713005706.mmc2.pdf on: 16-11-2013. Retrieved 16 November 2013.

Tager-Flusberg, H. and Joseph, R.M. (2003). Identifying neurocognitive phenotypes in autism. *Philosophical Transactions of the Royal Society of London B: Biological Sciences,* 358: 303–14.

Tager-Flusberg, H., Paul, R. and Lord, C. (2005). *Language and communication in autism*. In F. Volkmar, R. Paul, A. Klin and D.J. Cohen (eds.), *Handbook of Autism and Pervasive Developmental Disorders*. 3rd edition. New York: Wiley.

Tammet, D., (2007). *Born on a Blue Day: the gift of an extraordinary mind*. London: Hodder Paperback.

Tesink, C.M.J.Y., Buitelaar, J.K., Peterssona, K.M., van der Gaag, R.J., Teunissef, J-P. and Hagoort, P. (2011). Neural correlates of language comprehension in autism spectrum disorders: when language conflicts with world knowledge. *Neuropsychologia*, 49: 1095–1104.

Virtue, S., Parrish, T. and Jung-Beeman, M. (2008). Inferences during Story C Comprehension: cortical recruitment affected by predictability of events and working memory capacity. *Journal of Cognitive Neuroscience*, 20(12): 2274–84.

Wahlberg, T. and Magliano, J.P. (2004). The ability of high function individuals with autism to comprehend written discourse. *Discourse Processes*, 38(1): 119–44.

Wearing, C. (2010). Autism, metaphor and relevance theory. *Mind and Language*, 25(2): 196–216.

WHO (2007). *International Classification of Diseases and Related Health Problems*, Tenth Edition (ICD-10). Geneva: World Health Organization.

Wilkinson, K. and Twist, L. (2010). Autism and educational assessment: UK policy and practice. Slough: NFER. www.nfer.ac.uk/nfer/publications/ASR02/ASR02.pdf. Retrieved from Internet, 2 August 2011.

Williams, D. (1998). *Autism and Sensing: the unlost instinct.* London: Jessica Kingsley Publishers.

Wing, L. (1996, 2002). *The Autistic Spectrum.* New Updated Edition. London: Robinson.

Wing. L. and Shah, A. (2000). Catatonia in autistic spectrum disorders. *British Journal of Psychiatry*, 176: 357–62. http://bjp.rcpsych.org/ on March 24, 2013. Published by The Royal College of Psychiatrists. Retrieved from Internet, 24 March 2013.

Internet pages

Autism Education Trust: www.aettraininghubs.org.uk/wp-content/uploads/2012/06/AET-National-Autism-Standards_distributed.pdf
Graphic Novels: www.classicalcomics.com
Paley, S. (2013). Seclusion Rooms: A Parents' Guide: www.downssideup.com/2013/01/seclusion-rooms-parents-guide.html

Maps

www.freeusandworldmaps.com/html/WorldRegions/WorldRegionsPrint.html

ABC analysis

www.specialconnections.ku.edu/?q=behavior_plans/functional_behavior_assessment/teacher_tools/antecedent_behavior_consequence_chart
Social Stories and Comic Conversations by Carol Gray https://www.thegraycenter.org

Facebook page

Autism Discussion Page by Bill Nason, Psychologist. Describing, explaining and offering strategies to assist supporting children on the spectrum. https://www.facebook.com/autismdiscussionpage?fref=ts

YouTube videos

A is for Autism, BBC Four: www.youtube.com/watch?v=cPR2H4Zd8bl
www.sensory-processing-disorder.com/
Sensory Overload Simulation – WeirdGirlCyndi www.youtube.com/watch?v=BPDTEuotHe0
A Child's View of Sensory Processing – ESGWNRM www.youtube.com/watch?v=D1G5ssZlVUw
Derek Paravacini: Musical Genius
Daniel Tammet: The Boy with the Incredible Brain
Stephen Wiltshire draws a picture of Rome in 3 days: Beautiful Minds
BBC Newsround – My Autism and Me: Rosie www.youtube.com/watch?v=ejpWWP1HNGQ

Index

Entries in *italics* refer to titles of documents.